CONTEMPORARY'S

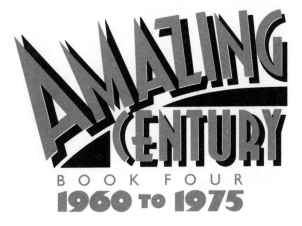

BOOK FOUR
1960 TO 1975

Developed by Contemporary Books, Inc., and General Learning Corporation, Northbrook, Illinois

Copyright © 1992 by Contemporary Books, Inc.
All rights reserved

No part of this publication may be reproduced, stored in a retrieval system, or transmitted in any form or by any means, without the prior written permission of the publisher.

Published by Contemporary Books, Inc.
180 North Michigan Avenue
Chicago, Illinois 60601
Manufactured in the United States of America
International Standard Book Number: 0-8092-4016-5

Published simultaneously in Canada by
Fitzhenry & Whiteside
91 Granton Drive
Richmond Hill, Ontario L4B 2N5
Canada

Library of Congress Cataloging-in-Publication Data

(Revised for vol. 4)

Amazing century.

  Includes indexes.
  Contents: bk. 1. 1900–1929 – bk. 2. 1929–1945 –
bk. 4. 1960–1975.
  1. United States – Civilization – 20th century.
2. Civilization, Modern – 20th century. I. Contemporary
Books, inc.
E169.1.A47186 1992   973.9   91-35292
ISBN 0-8092-4020-3 (pbk. : v. 1)
ISBN 0-8092-4018-1 (pbk. : v. 2)
ISBN 0-8092-4017-3 (pbk. : v. 3)

Editorial Director
Caren Van Slyke

Assistant Editorial Director
Mark Boone

Project Editor
Pat Fiene

Editorial
Chris Benton
Sarah Conroy

Editorial Production Manager
Norma Fioretti

Cover Design
Georgene Sainati

Cover Photo
Bettman Newsphotos

Executive Editor
Laura Ruekberg

Managing Editor
Alan Lenhoff

Associate Editor
Miriam Greenblatt

Assistant Editor
David Bristow

Art Director
Ami Koenig

Research
Sam Johnson
Therese Shinners
Betty Tsamis
Deborah Weise

To Our Readers

The civil rights "dream" of Dr. Martin Luther King, Jr. . . . Neil Armstrong's walk on the moon . . . the long, sad war in Vietnam . . . "Hammerin' Hank" Aaron's record-breaking home run . . . the coming of the hippies and the "Woodstock generation" . . .

In the pages of this book are some of the biggest news stories of their day. The photographs and stories in this book reach out to us. They tell about people and events that have helped to shape this century – and make our nation what it is today.

Though you may not know all the faces and places, you'll recognize many of the stories behind them. Today's triumphs and tragedies have their roots in the past – in the earlier years of this, our amazing century.

In pictures and in words, each of the books in the *Amazing Century* series highlights a different time period in this century. See for yourself. Thumb through the pages of this and all the *Amazing Century* books, and discover the way we were.

The Editors

Contents

TIMELINE

1961
23rd Amendment brings vote to D.C.

Soviet Yuri Gagarin is first space traveler

Bay of Pigs invasion fails

Alan B. Shepard, Jr., is first American in space

1964
24th Amendment does away with poll taxes

Civil Rights Act does away with Jim Crow laws

Tonkin Gulf Resolution passes Congress; Vietnam War heats up

1966
National Organization for Women (NOW) is founded

1963
President Kennedy is assassinated

Civil rights movement holds March on Washington

1967
Dr. Christiaan Barnard is first to do heart transplants

25th Amendment says who is next in line if president dies

1965
Black leader Malcolm X is assassinated

Voting Rights Act guarantees blacks' right to vote

34 die in Watts race riots

1960
Civil rights sit-in movement begins at Woolworth's in Greensboro, N.C.

1962
Cuban Missile Crisis occurs

34th–38th U.S. Presidents

Dwight Eisenhower	John Kennedy			Lyndon Johnson			
1960	1961	1962	1963	1964	1965	1966	1967

1969
Neil Armstrong
is first person
to walk on
moon

Woodstock
Music Festival
takes place in
New York

1973
U.S. signs
cease-fire and
withdraws
troops
from Vietnam

OPEC oil
embargo
triggers gas
shortage

Roe v. Wade
decision
legalizes
abortion
in all states

1971
26th
Amendment
lowers voting
age to 18

1968
Tet Offensive—
largest battle of
Vietnam War—
takes place

Dr. Martin
Luther King, Jr.,
is assassinated

Senator Robert
Kennedy is
assassinated

Antiwar protests
turn violent
during
Democratic
National
Convention
in Chicago

1970
NFL and AFL
unite
in new National
Football League

First Earth Day
marks new
awareness of
environmentalism

1974
President Nixon
resigns because
of Watergate
scandal

1972
Palestinian
terrorists
kill 11 Israeli
athletes at
Summer
Olympics

	Richard Nixon						Gerald Ford
1968	1969	1970	1971	1972	1973	1974	1975

The Torch Is Passed— Then Tragedy

President John F. Kennedy delivering his inaugural address—his first speech as president. Vice President Lyndon Johnson (front right) watches Kennedy speak.

It was January 20, 1961, in Washington, D.C. A blanket of snow lay on the ground. The wind howled. Even at noon, the temperature was below freezing. Yet 43-year-old John Fitzgerald Kennedy wore neither a hat nor a coat as he took the oath of office as president of the United States. Kennedy had a point to make. He was the youngest person ever elected to lead our nation. He was the first president born in the 20th century. He wanted to show the American people that a new generation, full of strength and energy, was about to lead the government. He set the tone of his presidency when he said:

> Let the word go forth from this time and place . . . that the torch has been passed to a new generation of Americans, born in this century, tempered by war, disciplined by a hard and bitter peace, proud of our ancient heritage. . . . Now the trumpet summons us again—not as a call to bear arms, though arms we need . . . but a call to bear the burden of . . . a struggle against the common enemies of man: tyranny, poverty, disease and war itself. . . . And so, my fellow Americans, ask not what your country can do for you; ask what you can do for your country.

The New Frontier

While running for president, Kennedy had promised to put into place new health, education, and civil rights programs. He had also promised to take a firm stand against Communist governments and to work to maintain America's position as the world's leading democratic nation. His plans were known as the "New Frontier."

During his time in office, Congress voted in some of his programs. It raised the minimum wage. It provided money to rebuild city slums. It voted for an ambitious space program to put an American on the moon before the end of the 1960s. But Congress voted down other programs, including aid to public schools and medical insurance for senior citizens.

The Bay of Pigs

Kennedy faced even greater challenges in foreign affairs. Relations between the United States and Cuba had been poor ever since Fidel Castro had become the leader of Cuba in 1959. Many Americans feared that Castro was creating a Communist state just 90 miles from U.S. shores.

During President Eisenhower's administration, the Central Intelligence Agency, or CIA, had made plans to invade Cuba. The invasion was to be carried out by a group of Cubans who had fled Castro's government and wanted to see Castro overthrown.

The Cubans were to land at the Bay of Pigs on Cuba's south coast and lead the Cuban people in a revolt against Castro. Kennedy was not sure that the plan was wise. But given his earlier promises to take a stand against the spread of communism, Kennedy decided to go ahead with the invasion.

He was soon sorry he had. The invasion, carried out in April 1961, was a complete failure. The Cuban people did not revolt against Castro, and the invaders were either killed or captured by the Cuban government.

The Cuban Missile Crisis

In the fall of 1962, an even greater crisis occurred. Again, Cuba was at the center. U.S. spy planes discovered that the Soviet Union had built several missile bases in Cuba. If missiles were installed there, they would be able to reach the United States in less than three minutes. The entire eastern and southern part of our nation would be in great danger.

Kennedy took action. On October 22, he announced that he was ordering U.S. Navy ships to surround Cuba and keep the Soviets from installing missiles there. He also demanded that the Soviet Union shut down the bases. Kennedy warned, "These actions may only be the beginning. . . . Any hostile move . . . will be met by whatever action is needed."

For almost a week, the world wondered whether World War III would break out. Then, on October 28, Soviet premier Nikita Khrushchev agreed to dismantle the bases. In return, the United States promised not to invade Cuba.

The Cuban Missile Crisis – and the threat of nuclear war – frightened the world. On August 5, 1963, the United States, her close ally Great Britain, and the Soviet Union signed a treaty to stop the testing of atomic weapons above ground or in the ocean. More than 100 other nations also signed the Nuclear Test Ban Treaty.

Tragedy in Dallas

By late 1963, Kennedy had enjoyed successes and suffered failures. He also had a presidential election coming up the next year. On November 22, he flew to Dallas, Texas, to deliver a political speech. As he rode in an open car through the city streets, three shots rang out. The president slumped in his seat. He was pronounced dead within the hour. Vice President Lyndon B. Johnson was sworn in as president. The whole nation mourned the death of its young leader.

That afternoon, Lee Harvey Oswald was arrested and charged with Kennedy's assassination. Two days later, Oswald himself was shot to death

A Soviet ship (top), carrying missiles on deck, being escorted away from Cuba by a U.S. warship after the Soviets agreed to remove the missiles. The Cuban Missile Crisis brought the two superpowers to the brink of war.

Three-year-old John Kennedy, Jr., saluting as his father's casket is carried past. Standing behind him are Jackie Kennedy, his mother, and Robert Kennedy, his uncle.

by Jack Ruby, a Dallas nightclub owner, while being taken from one jail to another. Millions of Americans saw the shooting on live TV.

Over the next several years, Johnson would carry out many of Kennedy's civil rights and antipoverty programs. He would, in fact, take them several steps further in an effort to wage "war on poverty" and to create "the Great Society." ■

People who supported the Bay of Pigs invasion believed that the United States was protecting its interests in Cuba and trying to prevent the spread of communism. People who were against the invasion said that it was wrong for the United States to interfere with another country's government. What is your opinion of the invasion? If you had been an adviser to President Kennedy, what would you have told him to do? Why?

Down with Segregation

In 1954, the Supreme Court ordered public schools to be integrated – made available to blacks as well as whites. Two years later, the U.S. Supreme Court said that public transportation also should be integrated. Still, other facilities in the South remained segregated – available either to whites only or to blacks only. In many southern towns and cities, Jim Crow laws said that blacks and whites could not drink from the same water fountains, stay at the same hotels, or play in the same parks. Then, in the 1960s, the movement to end segregation grew stronger.

Sit-Ins

The date was February 1, 1960. The place was an F. W. Woolworth store in Greensboro, North Carolina. Four black college students sat quietly at the lunch counter. They ignored the white youths who were throwing cigarette butts at them. The four blacks were waiting to be served coffee. But lunch counters in North Carolina were segregated. The counter was for whites only. So the store manager paid no attention to them.

The blacks came back the next day and the day after that. For the next two weeks, blacks staged similar "sit-ins" at Woolworth stores in 15 southern cities. At the same time, whites and blacks who opposed segregation picketed Woolworth stores in other parts of the United States.

The store managers tried to fight back. They removed lunch counter seats. They raised the price that they charged blacks for a cup of coffee from 5 cents to a dollar. Some managers even closed their lunch counters. But

their tactics failed. On July 25, the Woolworth store in Greensboro finally served coffee to blacks.

In the meantime, the sit-in movement had spread. The Student Nonviolent Coordinating Committee (SNCC) and other civil rights groups held sit-ins at libraries, movie theaters, beaches, and motels. John Lewis, Diane Nash, and other new leaders emerged.

Freedom Rides

The following year, 1961, the Congress of Racial Equality (CORE), under the leadership of James Farmer, used another nonviolent method to fight segregation. On May 4, seven blacks and six whites got on a bus in Washington, D.C., for a trip through the South. They called themselves "Freedom Riders." In town after town, they stopped at segregated bus stations to stretch their legs, grab a bite to eat, and use the bathrooms and barbershops. In many towns, they

Four college students during the second day of their 1960 sit-in at the Woolworth lunch counter in Greensboro, North Carolina.

were met by rocks, clubs, and bombs. But the movement spread, and other riders soon joined the original 13.

The local police did nothing to protect the Freedom Riders against attack. Finally, Attorney General Robert F. Kennedy, brother of President John Kennedy, sent in federal law officers to protect the protesters and maintain order. He also told the Interstate Commerce Commission, a U.S. government agency, to end segregation in bus stations, train depots, and airports. By the end of the year, "White" and "Colored" signs had disappeared from waiting rooms.

"I Have a Dream"

The last speaker of the March on Washington was Dr. Martin Luther King, Jr. The spirit of that day lives on in his speech. Some excerpts:

I have a dream that one day. . . the sons of former slaves and the sons of former slaveowners will be able to sit down together at the table of brotherhood. . . . I have a dream that my four little children will one day live in a nation where they will not be judged by the color of their skin but by the content of their character. . . . Let freedom ring. . . . And when this happens, when we allow freedom to ring, we will be able to speed up that day when all of God's children . . . will be able to join hands and sing in the words of the old Negro spiritual: "Free at last, free at last; thank God Almighty, we are free at last!"

Dr. Martin Luther King, Jr. (center), and other civil rights supporters during the 1963 March on Washington.

The March on Washington

In June 1963, President Kennedy sent a civil rights bill to Congress. On August 28, supporters of the bill—both blacks and whites—staged the March on Washington for Jobs and Freedom. The marchers' signs told what the bill was about:

- Effective Civil Rights Laws—Now!
- Integrated Schools—Now!
- Decent Housing—Now!

More than 200,000 people went to Washington, D.C. They sang hymns, such as "We Shall Overcome" and "Oh, Freedom." They listened to speeches. It was the largest demonstration of the civil rights movement. Members of CORE, SNCC, the Southern Christian Leadership Conference (SCLC), the National Association for the Advancement of Colored People (NAACP), and other groups attended. The marchers were sending a clear message to Congress: pass the bill.

On July 2, it did. The Civil Rights Act of 1964 said that schools, libraries, restaurants, and other public places must be integrated. It said employers could not refuse to hire people because of their race, color, religion, national origin, or sex. And it provided ways of protecting everyone's voting rights. ■

For many years, public washrooms, drinking fountains, and other facilities in the South carried signs that read "White" and "Colored." Imagine that you are a black growing up in the South at that time. How would the signs affect your opinion of whites? How would they affect your view of yourself?

Dr. Martin Luther King, Jr., was known as a powerful and inspiring speaker. His "I Have a Dream" speech is available on record and tape. Check your public library to see if it has a recording. Listening to King deliver his speech will give you a taste of what it was like at the March on Washington.

Cesar Chavez and the Grape Boycott

"Huelga, huelga!—strike, strike!"

Different groups of Americans used different techniques to call attention to their problems. During the 1960s, a Mexican-American farm worker named Cesar Chavez organized a union of migrant farm workers, called the United Farm Workers of America (UFWA). Migrant workers traveled from place to place picking crops. The work was part-time and low-paying. The workers lived in huts. They seldom had medical care. Children worked in the fields with their parents and were not sent to school. The farmworker's life was a hard one.

In 1965, the UFWA began a strike in California against the owners of farms that grew table grapes—grapes for eating. The union asked for higher wages and better working conditions. It also asked people throughout the United States to help by joining a grape boycott, that is, by not buying grapes. UFWA supporters picketed grocery stores.

The boycott worked. In 1970, the growers of more than half of California's table grapes signed contracts with the UFWA.

Long, Hot Summers

Many American cities were torn by rioting during the mid-1960s. Military troops patrol ravaged neighborhoods in the Watts area of Los Angeles.

The headlines read like this:
- 1965: 34 Die in Watts Ghetto Riots
- 1966: 43 Race Riots Erupt in Nation's Cities
- 1967: Newark Black Riots End After Six Days with 26 Dead
- 1967: Detroit Black Riots End After 8 Days, 43 Are Dead

By the mid-1960s, the civil rights movement had won some important victories. But many African-Americans were still out of work, still living in poverty, and still denied equal rights. Their patience had grown thin. Many continued to follow the nonviolent tactics of Dr. Martin Luther King, Jr. But others took to the streets. They were filled with rage over the nation's slow progress toward equal rights.

President Johnson set up a special group known as the Kerner Commission to look into the causes of the rioting. The commission had only bad news to report. It said what many Americans already knew: the standard of living in the nation's black ghettos was getting worse. The report summed up the situation by saying "Our nation is moving toward two societies—one black and one white—separate and unequal."

Some blacks supported the idea of separate societies. They believed that whites would never truly accept integration. They felt that blacks would be better off on their own. The Nation of Islam, better known as the Black Muslims, even proposed that a separate black nation be formed in the South, where the majority of blacks lived.

Other African-Americans supported

Malcolm X

Perhaps the strongest new militant black leader was Malcolm X. At the age of 21, he was sentenced to 10 years in prison for robbery. While in prison, he changed his life. He became a follower of Elijah Muhammad, leader of the Black Muslims. He taught himself to read by studying the dictionary, and he began reading his way through the prison library. In his autobiography, he wrote, "I knew right there in prison that reading had changed forever the course of my life. . . . The ability to read awoke inside me a craving to be mentally alive. . . . You will never catch me with a free fifteen minutes in which I'm not studying something I feel might be able to help the black man." Malcolm X was especially interested in black history. He felt that many blacks knew nothing about their past and culture because history books were written by and for whites.

Malcolm X took pride in black culture and wanted to teach others to do the same.

When Malcolm X got out of prison, he became a spokesperson for the Black Muslims. His devotion to black issues and his talent for public speaking won him many followers. In 1964, he left the Nation of Islam. He no longer believed that blacks should form their own nation, separate from whites. And he had lost faith in the leadership of the Black Muslims. He was a respected and powerful black leader in his own right when he was assassinated on February 21, 1965.

People took to the streets. They were filled with rage over the nation's slow progress toward equal rights.

the Black Power movement. Leaders of the movement pointed out that whites ran the government and owned most of the property and businesses in black communities. The movement called for blacks to work together to gain political and economic power of their own. Followers of the movement wanted blacks to own the businesses and run the schools in black neighborhoods. They wanted black police officers to patrol black communities. They urged blacks to vote for black candidates.

The Black Power movement had some successes. More blacks were elected to public office. More black police officers, fire fighters, and other public servants were hired. More blacks attended college, opening the door to better job opportunities. More blacks were featured in advertisements and on TV.

But many whites were frightened. They began to feel that the government was paying too much attention to blacks. They were afraid that if blacks gained, they would lose. Most of all, perhaps, they were scared by the riots that had broken out in cities all over the country. Many whites began to put law and order above everything else. ■

THE VIETNAM TRAP

Between 1961 and 1973, more than 3.3 million Americans served in Vietnam.

The Vietnam War was the longest and most unpopular war in American history. It was also the only war the United States ever lost.

Background File

The nations of Vietnam, Laos, and Cambodia used to be known as French Indochina. As the map on page 16 shows, they lay between India and China.

During the late 1800s, France took control of Indochina. Many Indo–Chinese resisted French rule. Among them were the parents of Ho Chi Minh. In 1912, Ho left Vietnam, his homeland, and sailed to Europe to escape arrest. During the early 1920s, Ho, inspired by the Russian revolution, became a Communist. He hoped to lead a revolution in Vietnam and overthrow the French. In Europe – and later in China – Ho attracted followers. When he returned to Vietnam, he built an army.

During World War II, Japanese soldiers took over Indochina. They left when the war ended. The French then tried to regain control. They fought Ho Chi Minh's army, the Vietminh, from 1946 to 1954. Communist China supported the Vietnamese. The United States and other Western powers supported France.

In 1954, the French admitted they had lost. That summer, a nine-nation conference was held at Geneva, Switzerland. Vietnam was divided into two parts. The Democratic Republic of Vietnam, or North Vietnam, was under

the control of the Vietminh. The Republic of Vietnam, or South Vietnam, was under the control of anti-Communists. It was agreed that in 1956 the Vietnamese would hold a national election to form a government for the entire country. Meanwhile, Laos and Cambodia had become independent nations – Laos in 1949, Cambodia in 1953.

When 1956 came, however, the

national election was not held. South Vietnam refused to take part. Why? Because Ngo Dinh Diem, South Vietnam's leader, realized that Ho would win.

Soon after, a rebellion broke out in South Vietnam. The rebels were called the Vietcong. Most Vietcong believed in one Vietnam. They wanted to reunify their country. But the Vietcong's leaders were Communists.

The United States began sending money and military advisers to South Vietnam in the 1950s. But in the early 1960s, the U.S. government began to take a larger role in Vietnam. America would soon find itself in a major war. Between 1961 and 1973, more than 3.3 million Americans served in Vietnam.

Kennedy's First Step

The Bay of Pigs had greatly embarrassed the United States. President Kennedy wanted to show the world that the United States would

stand firm against communism. By the time he was killed in 1963, he had sent 16,500 combat troops to South Vietnam as military "advisers." Two to three thousand more were ready, waiting to be sent.

Kennedy had also approved a plan to destroy the jungle where Vietcong rebels were hiding. This became known as Operation Ranch Hand. American planes began spraying poisonous chemicals, called *defoliants*, over South Vietnam. But the defoliants wiped out crops as well as trees. Soon, the South Vietnamese faced a shortage of rice, the main food in their diet.

After Kennedy died, the United States continued to expand the war.

North and South Vietnam (right). Left, Vietnam and southeast Asia.

Would Kennedy have added more troops if he had lived? Kennedy's advisers thought so. So did Lyndon Johnson, the new president.

Johnson's Free Hand
In August of 1964, President Johnson told Congress that North Vietnamese torpedo boats had attacked two U.S. ships in the Gulf of Tonkin, off the coast of North Vietnam. Johnson asked Congress to allow him to "take all necessary measures" to defend American forces in Vietnam and to prevent "further aggression." Later, investigators found that a mistake had been made and there had been no attacks. But by then, Congress had already passed the Gulf of Tonkin Resolution. In effect, it gave the president a "blank check" to fight a war in Vietnam.

A Bitter Conflict
In 1965, the United States began Operation Rolling Thunder. American planes bombed North Vietnam regularly—and heavily. The plan was to stop North Vietnamese troops and supplies from entering South Vietnam to help the Vietcong. Operation Rolling Thunder hurt the North Vietnamese, but it did not stop them.

The ground war was also growing rapidly. Less than a year earlier, President Johnson had promised voters that if he were reelected, he would not send American troops to fight in Vietnam. But by 1965, Johnson had committed 100,000 combat troops to the war.

In January of 1968, the Vietcong and the North Vietnamese began the largest battle of the war. It was known as the Tet Offensive because it had started during Tet, the Vietnamese New Year's holiday. The Vietcong and the North Vietnamese attacked more than 30 cities throughout Vietnam. After several weeks and many deaths, they were forced to retreat. By this time, however, it was clear that the United States and South Vietnam were not winning the war.

President Johnson did not run for reelection in 1968 – partly because he was so unpopular due to the war. Before he left office, he stopped the bombing of North Vietnam and set up peace talks with the Vietcong. But the talks went nowhere.

Nixon's Secret Plan

Richard M. Nixon was elected president in 1968. While he was running for office, he had promised to end the Vietnam War. He said he had a secret plan to obtain "peace with honor." The plan turned out to be a policy called *Vietnamization*. The United States would train the South Vietnamese to do all the fighting themselves so that American troops could gradually leave Vietnam.

American troops began returning home. At the same time, however, Nixon ordered the bombing of suspected Vietcong bases in Cambodia and Laos. American troops also raided Cambodia.

On January 27, 1973, the United States and North Vietnam finally signed a cease-fire agreement. Two months later, the last American soldiers left Vietnam. But the South Vietnamese were unable to hold off the North Vietnamese and the Vietcong by themselves. By April of 1975, Communist forces had gained control

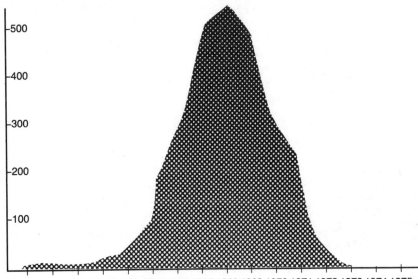

U.S. TROOPS IN VIETNAM
IN THOUSANDS

Source: U.S. Department of Defense

President Nixon announces that several thousand U.S. troops have entered Cambodia to attack Communist military bases.

of all of South Vietnam. Vietnam became a Communist nation.

A Balance Sheet

What were the costs of the war?

• Money: The United States spent $165 billion on the war. It sent South Vietnam $24 billion in aid between 1955 and 1975.

• Deaths: About 1.3 million people were killed. Almost 59,000 of these were Americans.

• Environment: About one-third of South Vietnam's countryside was destroyed.

• Refugees: The fighting forced about 9 million Indo-Chinese out of their homes. ■

Imagine that you are each of the following persons. What might you have thought about the Vietnam War during the 1960s?

• *An 18-year-old American boy about to be drafted*

• *A South Vietnamese rice farmer*

• *An American prisoner of war in North Vietnam*

The Vietnam Veterans Memorial has carved on its sides the names of all Americans who died or are missing in action in Vietnam.

THEN & NOW

It is probably the most popular monument in our nation's capital. Crowds of people come to see it. Some look at the list of names of all the Americans killed in Vietnam that is carved into the wall of the monument. Others gently touch an individual name. Some leave flowers in front of the black granite wall. More than a few weep.

Art student Maya Lin was just 20 years old when she designed the Vietnam Veterans Memorial, which was built in 1982. Until then, war memorials usually were figures of soldiers with their weapons. These memorials glorified war. As you can see from the picture, Maya Lin created something different — a new kind of war memorial. Lin wanted the living to have a chance to face the dead. She hoped it would help them overcome their grief. Thousands of relatives and friends of the dead soldiers visit the memorial each year.

Protest!

"**H**ey, hey, LBJ! How many kids did you kill today?"

Starting as early as 1963, Americans had begun protesting in public against the Vietnam War. Sometimes they marched around the White House and chanted slogans. Sometimes they tried to stop trains and buses carrying soldiers. College students and others staged sit-ins in public buildings and held large rallies. Several hundred draftees burned their draft cards. By 1968, about 10,000 Americans had fled to Canada to escape the draft.

At first, most of the protesters were young people. By 1968, however, the antiwar movement included Americans of all ages.

The 1968 Democratic Convention

"Stop the war!" shouted the youths.

"Keep law and order!" Chicago mayor Richard J. Daley told the police.

It was August 1968. The Democratic party was meeting in Chicago to pick its candidate for president of the United States. A rumor spread that 100,000 antiwar demonstrators were planning to come to the city and disrupt the Democratic convention. Daley was determined to stop them.

Daley turned Chicago into an armed camp. A barbed-wire fence went up around the convention hall. The police worked 12-hour shifts. The National Guard was called out. Even units of the U.S. Army stood ready to move in.

Antiwar protesters marching in Los Angeles in 1967.

Rioting in Chicago streets (top) during the 1968 Democratic convention. Antiwar protesters in Milwaukee, Wisconsin (bottom), burning bags of draft records that they stole from a Selective Service office.

As it turned out, only about 10,000 protesters showed up. Daley refused to give them permission to march or to hold rallies. He also ordered an 11 o'clock curfew in Lincoln Park, where many protesters were camping out.

The result was four nights of riots. Protesters who really did want trouble called the police "pigs" and threw stones and bottles at them. The police, in turn, used clubs and tear gas against all the protesters, even peaceful ones. Hundreds of people were injured. Six hundred protesters were arrested. And TV cameras recorded the riots for everyone to witness. Angry protesters chanted, "The whole world's watching; the whole world's watching." Many Americans were shocked and sickened by the violence in the streets.

Kent State

In May 1970, students at Kent State University in Kent, Ohio, were angry about the U.S. government's invasion of Cambodia. After two days of campus riots, the Ohio governor ordered that the students not be allowed to gather in groups until things calmed down. But the next day, May 4, students held a noon rally on a grassy area called the

Commons. At first, all was peaceful. Then, two jeeps filled with National Guardsmen appeared. "Evacuate the Commons area," the guardsmen shouted through bullhorns. A group of students threw stones. The guardsmen fired tear gas at the crowd and then retreated up a hill.

The guardsmen stood for a minute at the top of the hill. They carried repeating rifles with live ammunition. The students milled around at the foot of the hill. Most were hundreds of feet away, too far to harm the guardsmen.

Suddenly, a group of eight to 10 guardsmen knelt and fired their rifles. There was a moment's silence. Then a student screamed, "My God, they're killing us!"

They were indeed. The guardsmen fired 35 shots at the students. When they stopped, four students lay dead. Nine others were wounded.

President Nixon appointed a commission to look into the matter. It reported that the trouble began when the National Guard tried to break up the rally. Firing rifles into a crowd of unarmed students, said the commission, was "unnecessary" and "inexcusable." In 1974, eight of the guardsmen were tried for the deaths of the four students. All eight were found not guilty. ■

A Kent State student lies dead from the bullet of a National Guardsman. Another student looks on with horror.

Many of the protests of the 1960s were marked by violence. Do you think that violence helps or hurts a cause? Does keeping law and order mean preventing protests? What can a government do to keep law and order but at the same time allow protests?

Most public libraries carry back issues of newspapers and magazines. To see how people of the 1960s felt about protests against the Vietnam War, read news stories of the times.

Assassinations

April 4, 1968. Memphis, Tennessee. The sniper raised his rifle and looked through the scope. He fired one shot. It entered the neck of Dr. Martin Luther King, Jr., cutting his spinal column. An hour later, King was dead.

The murder touched off a nationwide explosion of rioting, looting, and setting of fires by blacks. In all, 168 cities in 29 states were struck. The worst hit was the nation's capital. There, 711 fires were set, and 10 people were killed. President Johnson called out the army and the National Guard to protect the city. Soldiers with bayonets surrounded the White House. A machine-gun post was set up on the steps of the Capitol. Nationwide, more than 2,600 fires were set; 46 people were killed, and more than 21,000 people were injured. It took 55,000 soldiers to restore order.

On June 5, another man fired a gun, this time at point-blank range. The victim was Robert F. Kennedy, who had just won the California primary election in his race for the Democratic nomination for president. Several more shots wounded five other persons. Kennedy died the next day.

A mule-drawn cart carries the casket of Dr. Martin Luther King, Jr., to his funeral.

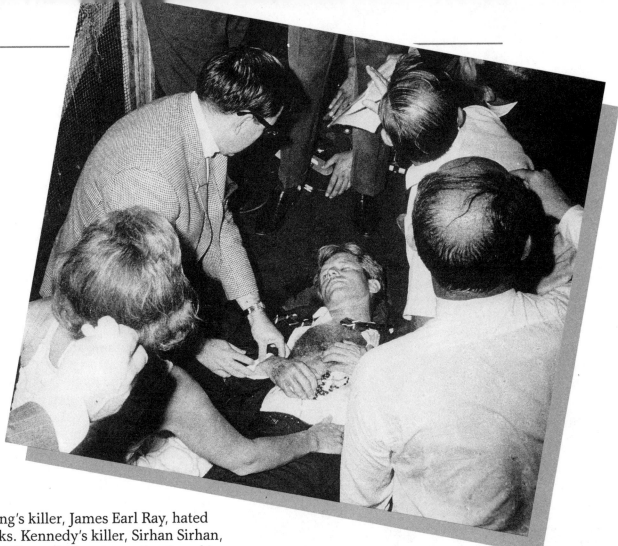

King's killer, James Earl Ray, hated blacks. Kennedy's killer, Sirhan Sirhan, hated Kennedy for supporting Israel in its conflicts with the Arabs of the Middle East.

Twice in two months, acts of violence had brought the nation into crisis. In addition, there were ongoing protests against racism, the Vietnam War, and economic problems. To many people, it seemed as if the United States were coming unglued. In November 1968, Americans decided that the way to solve the nation's problems was to change direction. They elected as president a man who said he would restore law and order: Richard M. Nixon. ■

No Toy Guns

Children whose parents shopped at Sears did not find toy guns under the Christmas tree in 1968. The company removed toy guns from its catalog after Dr. Martin Luther King, Jr., and Robert Kennedy were assassinated. The company also ordered its 815 stores to stop advertising toy guns. Toy companies and other retail stores throughout the country followed Sears' example.

Two months after the assassination of Dr. Martin Luther King, Jr., another gunman killed presidential candidate Robert Kennedy.

Most Americans are upset over the large number of people who are shot to death each year. Some people believe that one way to reduce the number of killings is through gun control—regulating or stopping the purchase of handguns. Other people argue that they have the right to defend themselves and that limiting the sale of guns will hurt law-abiding citizens more than criminals. What do you think?

The Watergate Scandal

The Watergate, the site of the break-in that led to the downfall of President Nixon.

"**P**eople have got to know whether or not their president is a crook. Well, I'm not a crook." So said Richard M. Nixon in November of 1973. Why did the president feel he had to say something like that? The answer lay in the Watergate scandal.

"A Third-Rate Burglary"?

President Nixon, a Republican, was running for reelection in 1972. On June 17, five men were caught breaking into the Washington, D.C., offices of the Democratic party. The offices were in the Watergate, a large group of apartment houses and office buildings. The burglars carried wiretapping and photographic equipment. They also carried papers linking them with the Committee to Re-elect the President (CREP). Given the evidence, the burglars seemed to be spies collecting information about the Democrats. The information could be used to help Nixon beat his Democratic opponent in the race for the presidency. Nixon said that he knew nothing about the men or the break-in. In fact, Nixon's spokesman tried to make the break-in seem unimportant by referring to it as "a third-rate burglary."

The Watergate burglars went on trial before Judge John J. Sirica early in 1973. Also on trial for playing a part in the break-in were E. Howard Hunt, Jr., a White House aide, and G. Gordon Liddy, a lawyer for CREP. Liddy and James W. McCord, Jr., one of the burglars, were convicted. The other men pleaded guilty.

The Scandal Unfolds

At the sentencing, Sirica read aloud a letter from McCord. It said that the defendants had lied in court; the White House had known all along about the break-in and was trying to hide the truth. Sirica put off sentencing McCord so that McCord could answer questions during upcoming Senate hearings on the Watergate affair. Then Sirica sentenced the other defendants to long prison terms, saying that he would review the sentences in three months.

Senate hearings began in May 1973. Millions of Americans watched them on TV. In July, they learned that Nixon had tape-recorded many of his conversations with staff members. The Senate committee asked to hear the tapes. Nixon refused. Sirica ordered Nixon to produce the tapes. Nixon still refused.

From Bad to Worse

The battle over the Watergate tapes continued. In October, Nixon finally agreed to turn over a few. But one was incomplete. It contained an 18½-minute gap. Apparently, part of the recording of a conversation had been erased.

By this time, the House Judiciary Committee was also investigating Watergate. Under the U.S. Constitution, it is the duty of the House of Representatives to decide whether a president can be impeached – charged with misconduct – and then removed from office.

In July 1974, the Supreme Court ruled unanimously that Nixon had to turn over all the tapes. Not even the president is above the law, said the Court. The same month, the House Judiciary Committee passed a bill to impeach the president.

Nixon Resigns

On August 5, Nixon finally released the tapes. They showed that he had, after all, known all about Watergate from the start. He had lied to Congress and to the American people.

Events moved swiftly. On August 8, Nixon announced that he was resigning his office. He was the first president in American history to do so. On August 9, Gerald Ford, vice president under Nixon, became president. On September 8, 1974, President Ford pardoned Nixon of "all offenses against the United States." ■

Ford's pardon of Nixon was a topic of debate in many American homes. Those in favor of the pardon said that Nixon had already suffered enough by being forced to resign. Those against the pardon said that Nixon had broken the law and had to be punished. What do you think? If you were Ford, would you have pardoned Nixon? Why or why not?

Nixon giving his farewell speech on August 9, 1974.

Revolution on Campus

Some kids felt a sense of urgency about working for political change.

"That Bomb Has Got to Go"..."If You Miss Me from the Back of the Bus"..."Blowin' in the Wind"..."There but for Fortune"..."Little Boxes"...

In the early 1960s, folk protest songs like these were sung in the dark, smoky little coffeehouses that seemed to be in every U.S. college town. Folk was *the* music on campus – at least among the serious-minded. Pete Seeger, Malvina Reynolds, Joan Baez, Bob Dylan, Phil Ochs, Judy Collins – these folksingers and others were idols to the young. Kids weren't just lining up to see them; they were trying to be them. For a time, it seemed as if every high school and college had its would-be Joan Baezes, its Bob Dylan copycats.

What made folk protest music so popular? Folk touched on issues that mattered to the young. Many kids were taking a hard look at their country, and they did not like what they saw.

In the News

Students were reading Michael Harrington's *The Other America*, a book about widespread poverty in the United States. TV, newspapers, and magazines carried shocking reports of southern whites' attacks on southern blacks. The Cuban Missile Crisis was still fresh in students' minds. So was the fallout-shelter movement. Worried about the threat of war with the Soviet Union, President Kennedy had urged Americans to add bomb shelters to their homes. Nuclear war didn't seem like a faraway threat; it seemed like something that could happen here – at any moment.

Some kids felt a sense of urgency about working for political change. As the editor of Stanford University's student newspaper put it in 1963, "We are children of a time of ferment [great trouble], and as historical beings we make the ferment ours."

The civil rights movement was setting an example. It showed that people could make a difference by working together for social justice. Kids also were inspired by their young president, John Kennedy. He had seemed to speak directly to them when he said "ask what you can do for your country." Many *were* asking what they could do – about poverty, nuclear arms, segregation, and other problems that they saw. Some had already begun to take action.

The SDS

A "New Left" – that was the dream of University of Michigan students Al Haber and Tom Hayden. The two were leaders of a campus political group called the Students for a Democratic Society (SDS). They hoped to unite students, workers, minority groups, and the poor into a movement working for political change.

What changes did the SDS want? An end to the nuclear arms race between the United States and the Soviet Union. Equal rights for blacks. Programs to help the poor. An end to capitalism, which, the SDS felt, put money and power in the hands of a few.

To idealistic kids out to change the world, the SDS was new, exciting, and serious about social justice. Soon, students at other colleges and universities set up their own SDS groups.

In 1963, the SDS began its Economic Research and Action Project. Members of the project set up offices in several U.S. cities. There, the SDS organized the poor into political action groups pushing for better housing, jobs, and city services.

As the SDS was working to build its New Left, another movement was building. It, too, started on college campuses.

The Free Speech Movement

"There's a time when the operation of the machine . . . makes you so sick at heart that you can't take part.
. . . You've got to indicate to the people who run the machine . . . that unless you're free, the machine will be prevented from working at all."

The speaker was student Mario Savio. The place was the University of California, Berkeley. And the machine was the university itself. As Savio spoke, a crowd of 1,000 cheered him on. Among them was Joan Baez. She sang "We Shall Overcome" as Savio and the others marched into Sproul Hall and held a sit-in.

At issue was the university's right to control students' political activity. The university said that students could not use school property to announce political actions like strikes or sit-ins — even if these actions were to take place off campus. Savio and the others complained that students were being treated like second-class citizens. All Americans are guaranteed freedom of speech, they argued. They demanded that the university treat students as equals. The students wanted a say in

Members of the Students for a Democratic Society march toward the White House on Election Day, 1968.

Dylan

Dylan's songs put into words what many kids were feeling.

In 1961, Bob Dylan made the scene at Gerde's Folk City, a popular coffeehouse in New York. In folk music circles, it was a sign that he had arrived.

Kids were going wild for Dylan. He made old folk music sound completely new. He didn't sing it; he growled it, screamed it, howled it, whispered it. He played the guitar and harmonica with the same raw emotion.

Dylan's songs put into words what many kids were feeling. "Blowin' in the Wind" was a quiet, simple song against war. "A Hard Rain's A-Gonna Fall" was a brooding song about people's indifference to war, poverty, and other world problems. "The Times They Are A-Changin' " was a soaring song about the growing spirit of activism among the young. In it, Dylan warned parents that their children were beyond their command. It was one of the first songs about the clash between young and old in the 1960s. Songs like these earned Dylan the title "spokesperson for a generation."

their education and in decisions affecting campus life. The sit-in was their way of fighting for greater political power. During the overnight sit-in on December 2–3, 1964, the free speech movement was born.

The university told the students to leave the building. Again and again, they refused. Finally, California governor Edmund Brown ordered the police to remove them. Following the example of civil rights activists, the students let their bodies go limp as the police came to take them away.

It took police 12 hours to drag the students from the building. More than 800 were arrested. The sit-in made national news. So did the strike that students held over the next few days. Many students – and some teachers – supported the strike and refused to attend classes. As a result, the university changed its rules, and students won a greater voice in university government.

The Movement Spreads

After the protest at Berkeley, students at other schools began pressing for changes at their universities. They began demanding representation on their universities' governing boards. They pushed for classes on issues important to African-Americans, women, and other minorities. They wanted their schools to drop dress codes – rules about "proper" dress in the dorms. They protested against curfews – rules saying how late students could stay out at night. Guys and girls demanded the right to visit each other in their dorm rooms whenever they wanted – even overnight. What had started as a protest at Berkeley was growing into something America had never seen before – a nationwide movement for student power.

A Generation Gap

During the height of the Berkeley sit-in, activist Jack Weinberg was reported to have warned protesters, "Don't trust anyone over 30." His statement was becoming as famous as the Berkeley protest itself. By the mid-1960s, there was a new spirit of rebellion among the young. Kids and adults didn't seem to see eye to eye on anything. Newspapers and magazines called the clash between young and old a "generation gap." More and more kids were questioning the "Establishment"—their parents' lifestyles, beliefs, and values.

Drug use was becoming more common on campus. Some kids said that blowing weed—smoking marijuana—was harmless fun. Kids' attitude toward sex also was changing. Once, "nice" kids had frowned on sex before marriage. Now, it was becoming the norm. Unspoken rules against swearing were falling by the wayside. Some adults complained that the free speech movement had turned into the foul speech movement.

But to some Americans, the most alarming trend of all was students' changing attitude toward the war in Vietnam. A growing number of kids were joining the antiwar movement.

A New Direction

The movement against the war gave student political groups like the SDS a new sense of purpose and direction. In the antiwar movement, the SDS found like-minded kids and adults. The SDS had long been against the arms race. Joining the antiwar movement was a natural next step.

It also was a small step from the free speech movement to the antiwar movement. To some kids, the war was yet another example of young people's powerlessness. The government had the right to draft 18-year-olds into the army and send them to serve in Vietnam. Yet 18-year-olds did not have the right to vote against the leaders who were sending them there. Ending the war became part of students' drive for political power.

Teach-Ins and Marches

Early demonstrations against the war were peaceful. Protesters were filled with a sense of hope. In the mid-1960s, many in the antiwar movement believed that the government would end the war quickly if enough

The free speech movement demanded greater political power for students.

Americans came out against U.S. involvement in Vietnam.

On many college campuses, professors and student leaders held "teach-ins"—discussions to educate people about America's involvement in Vietnam. One of the largest was Vietnam Day, held over the weekend of May 21, 1965, at the University of California, Berkeley. Many famous and soon-to-be famous antiwar leaders spoke. Student Jerry Rubin, who had helped organize the teach-in. Dr. Benjamin Spock, a leader of the National Committee for a Sane Nuclear Policy (SANE) and popular author of child-care books. Longtime activist David Dellinger, editor of *Liberation*

Many antiwar professors and students held "teach-ins" about America's involvement in Vietnam.

magazine. Robert Moses, an organizer of the civil rights movement. Senator Ernest Gruening, one of the first members of Congress to come out against the war.

Several large, peaceful demonstrations also took place in 1965. The SDS led the first national protest against the war, the April 17 March on Washington. More than 20,000 took part. On October 15–16, protests and teach-ins were held across the United States in honor of the First International Day of Protest. The antiwar movement was growing.

Hell, No, We Won't Go!

By 1966, the antidraft movement also was growing. As the United States became more involved in Vietnam, the armed forces needed more troops. In response, the Selective Service System—the group in charge of the draft—changed its rules. In the past, full-time students had been exempt (excused) from the draft. Now, full-time students who did not make good grades could be drafted. The change sparked protests from both universities and their students.

Some professors complained that grades had become a matter of life and death. If they flunked male students, the students might be drafted and sent to Vietnam. Students held antidraft protests on several college campuses. Kids chanting "Hell, no, we won't go!" marched in front of their local draft boards. Students also held "burn-ins" and "turn-ins"—protests in which they burned their draft cards or mailed them back to their draft boards.

In Minnesota, Barry Bondhus broke into the offices of a local draft board and destroyed hundreds of draft records. About a year and a half later, Catholic priests Philip and Daniel Berrigan made national news when they were arrested for burning draft

records in Catonsville, Maryland. Other antidraft protests followed these examples.

Which Side Are You On?

Though the antiwar movement was gathering force, polls in 1967 showed that most Americans still supported U.S. involvement in Vietnam. Disagreements about the war were intense and emotional. "Hawks"—Americans in favor of the war—believed that protests were unpatriotic. They could not believe that the younger generation—children of Americans who had served in World War II—would burn their draft cards or refuse to serve their country. "Doves"—Americans against the war—argued that World War II had been different. Germany and Japan had invaded peaceful nations. The conflict in Vietnam, they said, was a civil war—a clash between groups of people fighting for control of their own country.

Demonstrations against the war spread. On college campuses, students protested against the Reserve Officers Training Corps (ROTC), which trains young people to be officers in the armed services. They also protested against recruiters for the armed services, the CIA, and the Dow Chemical Company. Dow made napalm, a chemical that was being used to burn away Vietcong jungle hideouts. At the same time, napalm was burning and killing Vietnamese men, women, and children. In October 1967, a sit-in against a Dow office at the University of Wisconsin turned violent. For the first time, police used tear gas to break up a campus protest.

Over the weekend of October 20, more than 50,000 protesters gathered at the Lincoln Memorial in Washington, D.C., and marched to the Pentagon—the headquarters of the U.S.

armed services. When some protesters broke away and tried to storm the building, they, too, were met with tear gas.

Dark Days

By the late 1960s, infighting was occurring in the antiwar movement, the student movement, and the civil rights movement. Most activists still believed in working "within the system"—using nonviolent protests, the vote, and other lawful methods to

Catholic priests Philip (left) and Daniel Berrigan were arrested for burning draft records.

make their voice heard. But others felt that nonviolence had gotten them nowhere. Hope gave way to anger.

In 1968, riots exploded in many cities after the assassination of Dr. Martin Luther King, Jr. Shortly after King died, Robert Kennedy, who was running for president on an antiwar platform, was assassinated. Remembering the violence of the time, Carl Oglesby, an ex-leader of the SDS, spoke for many when he said, "What do you do? Get a new hero?. . . People started talking about revolution, because reform had been made to seem like a dead-end street."

In April and May 1968, Columbia University in New York City was rocked by demonstrations; more than 100 students were hurt. In August 1968, protests at the Democratic National Convention in Chicago turned into riots. Chicago was again hit by violence in October 1969. The Weathermen—a radical group that had split from the SDS—broke windows, smashed cars, and attacked police and bystanders in the "Days of Rage." In May of 1970, four students were killed by National Guardsmen in protests at Kent State University in Ohio. Also in May, two students were killed in protests at Jackson State University in Mississippi. In August 1970, protesters at the University of Wisconsin bombed Sterling Hall, home of the Army Math Research Center. A young scientist was killed.

Most in the antiwar movement were horrified by the violence. They wanted peace—both at home and in Vietnam. So did most Americans. By the late 1960s, public opinion had turned against the war. In October 1969, thousands of Americans across the United States took part in Moratorium Day—24 hours of peaceful antiwar rallies, marches, and teach-ins. In November, 250,000 antiwar protesters held the biggest rally in the history of the nation's capital.

The Pentagon Papers

As the war dragged on, America was hit with more shocking news. In June 1971, the *New York Times* printed the "Pentagon Papers"—a secret government report about Vietnam. Daniel Ellsberg, who had helped write the report, gave it to the newspaper because he felt the information should be made public. The report showed that in many cases the government had not told the American people the truth about U.S. involvement in Vietnam.

In January 1973, a cease-fire agreement ended U.S. military involvement in Vietnam. But the "credibility gap" lived on. After the Pentagon Papers, many Americans no longer believed what their government told them. Distrust was one of the many sad outcomes of the war in Vietnam. ■

If you were to write a new version of "The Times They Are A-Changin' " for the 1990s, what would your song be about?

Bob Dylan was called the "spokesperson for a generation." Who are spokespersons for the younger generation today? What messages do they have for young people?

The Women's Movement

"Go Home!" a man yelled at a group of protesters in front of Convention Hall, Atlantic City. "Only an insane person would do something like this!" shouted a woman. Was it another antiwar rally? Another protest against the draft? No, it was a kind of demonstration that many had never seen before. It was the Women's Liberation Front, protesting against the 1968 Miss America Pageant and society's attitude toward women.

"I Am a Woman – Not a Toy, a Pet, or Mascot," said a sign carried by one protester. "No More Beauty Standards – Everyone Is Beautiful," read another. The women drew insults – and a few laughs – when they threw makeup, bras, girdles, and high-heeled shoes into a "freedom trash can." Their action was a typical 1960s "zap" – a way of drawing attention to a cause. The zap worked. The women's liberation movement made national news.

What was the women's liberation movement, and what did it hope to achieve? The movement was made up of feminist (women's rights) groups from across America. Many were small, informal neighborhood or campus groups in which women held "rap sessions" – discussions – to "raise their consciousness" – discover their feelings about themselves as women. Though each group was different, all shared a goal – to change America's ideas about what women could and should be.

Wives and Mothers

In the early 1960s, most people thought that women should concentrate on being wives and mothers. In 1962, the *Saturday Evening Post* magazine summed up a survey of women by saying that "the American female has strongly rooted purpose. It's home and family – motherhood." The *Post* survey supported a view of women that had long been held. But a growing number of women felt that being a wife and mother was not enough. One of these women was Betty Friedan.

The Voice Within

Friedan's 1963 book, *The Feminine Mystique*, was a surprise hit. In the book, Friedan argued that many stay-at-home mothers were secretly unhappy with their lives. She said that the women were dissatisfied because they lived only through their husbands and children.

The Women's Liberation Front made headlines by protesting the 1968 Miss America Pageant.

What did women need? Meaningful work, Friedan said – the same kind of work that gives men satisfaction. She wrote, "We can no longer ignore that voice within women that says, 'I want something more than my husband and my children and my home.'"

National Organization for Women

In 1966, Friedan helped start the National Organization for Women (NOW). NOW's main goal was to pass the Equal Rights Amendment (ERA) – an addition to the U.S. Constitution that would guarantee women equal rights. NOW also wanted paid leave for women employees who take time off from work to have a baby and low-cost daycare centers for working parents. And NOW wanted abortion to be made legal throughout the United States.

NOW Is Not Enough

Some women felt that NOW did not go far enough. In the 1970 book *Sisterhood Is Powerful*, Robin Morgan called for an end to the "nuclear family unit" – a family in which the man earns a living while the woman raises the children and runs the home. Morgan said that this type of family puts a woman "into a totally dependent position, paying for her keep with . . . labor which is not even considered work."

In *Sexual Politics*, Kate Millett said that women were held back by a society run by and for men. Just as whites had kept blacks from achieving all that they could, so men were keeping women from being all that they could be.

Australian feminist Germaine Greer added to the outcry with her book *The Female Eunuch*. Greer argued for greater sexual freedom, an end to marriage, and an end to the nuclear family. She wrote, "The first discovery that we shall make as we rocket along our female road to freedom is that men are not free, and they will seek to make this an argument why nobody should be free. We can only reply that . . . by securing our [freedom] we may show men the way they could follow. . . ."

The early 1970s were active years for the women's movement. In 1970, Friedan led a nationwide protest, the Women's Strike for Equality. In 1971, some women in the movement began the National Women's Political Caucus, a group working to end "sexism, racism, violence, and poverty." Many of the best-known names in the women's movement were on the board. U.S. Representatives Bella S. Abzug and Shirley Chisholm. Betty Friedan. Writer Gloria Steinem. The first nationwide feminist magazine, Gloria Steinem's *Ms.*, also appeared in 1971.

Not for Everyone

As the women's liberation movement got more notice, it also gained more enemies. Professor Lionel Tiger, archenemy of the movement, wrote article after article "proving" that women were, by nature, unable to be leaders. Some women formed anti-liberation groups such as the Pussycats. Their motto? "The lamb chop is mightier than the karate chop." Groups like the Pussycats were hard to take seriously. But many people – men and women alike – had serious arguments against the movement.

Some people felt that women's traditional roles – wife and mother – were important to the country. They believed that the movement was hurting family life. And many stay-at-home mothers felt that the movement was insulting them, saying that their work as homemakers wasn't valuable.

But the movement did change many people's lives in important ways. Whether or not people liked the movement, they could not avoid the questions it raised – questions about women's roles in the family and the nation. The United States would never go back to *assuming* that women belonged only in the home. The movement had given women new freedom of choice. ■

Feminist Gloria Steinem, one of the founders of *Ms.* magazine.

Some people feel that the women's liberation movement hurt family life. They believe that women with young children should not work. What do you think?

Feminists called for women to come up with new structures for the family. In your opinion, what is the ideal family structure? Why?

THEN & NOW

In 1960, women earned only about 60 cents for every dollar men earned. In 1963, the U.S. Congress took steps to help working women when it passed the Equal Pay Act. The law said that employers must pay women the same amount as men for jobs that require the same "skill, effort, and responsibility." But the law didn't cover all types of jobs. Also, people who worked for many years at a job (usually men) were still paid more than new employees (often women). So the law did not have much effect on women's pay overall.

Has the gap between women's and men's wages narrowed since the 1960s? Yes it has – but only recently. By 1989, women were earning 70 cents for every dollar earned by men.

What happened? According to Professor June O'Neill of Baruch College, the large number of women who began working in the 1960s and 1970s held down the average wage for women. O'Neill says that before 1960 the few women who worked were well educated and had strong skills. But the women who entered the work force during the 1960s didn't have the same kinds of skills or experience.

This situation changed in the 1980s, O'Neill says. As schooling and job skills have improved, so have women's wages. O'Neill thinks the true wage gap between men and women with equal skill and experience is now less than 10 percent.

Far Out!

It was a time of breaking loose, slamming the door on the past, letting it all hang out, doing your own thing. It was the era of free love, long hair, psychedelic drugs, and Woodstock. It was a time when many kids became, as a spokesperson for the young put it, "the people our parents warned us against." It was the second half of the 1960s, one of the wilder times the nation had ever seen.

Hippies developed new styles. They didn't want to look like middle-class people.

The Flower Children

The hippie movement was in full swing. In San Francisco's Haight-Ashbury neighborhood, the summer of 1967 was the "summer of love." Some 50,000 kids crowded into the 44-block area to live, for a time, the life of a hippie. At the same time, hippie neighborhoods were going strong in other major cities. Hippies roamed the streets of New York City's East Village and camped out in Tompkins Square Park. In Boston, hippies hung out on the Common and romped in Frog Pond. In Chicago's Old Town, Wells Street was the hippie place to be.

The "flower children," as hippies were sometimes called, had turned their backs on middle-class America. Parents were telling their sons and daughters to find someone nice, get married, and settle down. Hippies were saying it was better to find nice people and settle down in communes — groups of guys and girls living together. Parents told their kids to get good jobs and make good money. Abbie Hoffman said, "Burn your money and be free!" Parents said, "Only dopes use dope." Dr. Timothy Leary, ex–Harvard psychology professor, said, "Turn on, tune in, drop out, and follow me." His International Foundation for Internal Freedom (IF-IF) had helped to make psychedelic drugs like LSD popular.

Leary said that dropping acid — taking LSD — would take people on sensational trips out of their minds. They would, he said, experience fantastic sights and sounds and wild flights of the imagination. He also said that LSD would help people find God. For Leary, LSD and other drugs were ways to open the mind to the spiritual.

Ken Kesey, writer of *One Flew Over the Cuckoo's Nest,* also had helped make LSD popular. In the spring of 1964, he and a group of his friends – the Merry Pranksters – had driven across America in a brightly painted old school bus. Along the way, they held "acid tests" – parties in which they passed out LSD to new users. Along with drugs, the parties featured rock music and light shows. Drugs, music, and colorful flashing lights were all part of the psychedelic experience – an attempt to trick the senses into seeing the world in a totally new way.

Psychedelia

Psychedelia was in. Hip New Yorkers hung out at dance spots like the Fillmore East, the Group Image, and the Electric Circus. As they listened to the latest rock, they also experienced light shows that went steps beyond the "acid tests." Strobe lights flashed on and off, making dancers look as if they were moving in slow motion. Black lights made psychedelic posters glow eerily in the dark. A slide projector sent swirling shapes, bright colors, and crazy pictures floating on the ceiling, the walls, the floor, the stage, and the dancers.

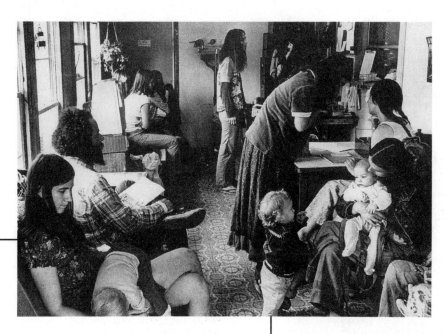

Life on a Commune

A small community in which everyone felt like one big family. A community in which everyone took part in decisions affecting community life. A community in which no one was richer or poorer than anyone else. A community of sharing. That was the dream behind many hippie communes of the 1960s and early 1970s.

Some hippies shared houses, setting up communes in the cities. Others set up communes in the country, such as Morningstar, near San Sebastopol, California.

Morningstar was located on a ranch owned by Lou Gottlieb, a member of the folksinging group the Limeliters. In 1966, Gottlieb opened his ranch to Haight-Ashbury hippies, calling it "open land." Depending on the time of year, from 30 to 100 people lived at the commune.

There were few rules. While some used drugs, others believed in getting high naturally. "The sun is my trip," one Morningstar hippie told a reporter. "I can turn on just watching the glint on the edges of the needles [of redwood trees]."

The people of Morningstar grew organic (chemical-free) vegetables on the ranch and shared them with hippies in Haight-Ashbury. They believed in returning to the land and what they saw as a simpler, more natural way of life.

This commune, which was called the "Farm," had its own health clinic.

Members of the Krishna Society (above) chant and dance in downtown Minneapolis. Rock singer Janis Joplin (right) in concert.

At the Fillmore in San Francisco, kids flocked to see the hottest bands—the Doors, the Jefferson Airplane, the Grateful Dead, Buffalo Springfield, Big Brother and the Holding Company, with lead singer Janis Joplin belting out a soulful blues.

East Meets West

Eastern religions and culture also were in. Americans in search of inner peace were looking into Zen Buddhism from Japan, Hinduism from India, Taoism from China. Words that had once seemed strange to American ears were used in everyday conversations—ashrams (Hindu religious communities), mantras (words believed to have a magical power to relax the mind), gurus (Hindu spiritual leaders), shamans (Asian—and American Indian—priests).

In December 1965, the Beatles' "Norwegian Wood" had introduced many Americans to the sitar—a stringed instrument from India. Soon after, the sitar could be heard on the Rolling Stones' hit "Paint It Black." By the late 1960s, sitar master Ravi Shankar was almost as familiar to American kids as the Beatles. So was the Maharishi Mahesh Yogi. The Beatles helped make the spiritual leader famous when they traveled to India to study with him.

The Woodstock Music Festival

For some kids, the high point of the late 1960s was the Woodstock Music Festival. In August 1969, 500,000 kids traveled to a 600-acre farm in upstate New York for the outdoor concert. For three days, they listened, sang along, danced, clapped, laughed, drank beer, smoked pot, and camped out.

Many of the biggest rock stars of the era made the scene. Jimi Hendrix blew away the crowd with his electric version of "The Star-Spangled Banner." Country Joe and the Fish sang the biggest antiwar song of the day, "I-Feel-Like-I'm-Fixin'-to-Die Rag." David Crosby, Stephen Stills, and Graham Nash nervously took the stage together for the first time.

Newspaper, magazine, and TV reporters had a field day when kids stripped off their clothes to dance and bathe in a pond on the farm. Cameras were rolling to record the biggest love-in of them all. ■

Two very different movies give a good picture of the hippie lifestyle: Alice's Restaurant *(1969) and the documentary* Woodstock *(1970).*

Some people think that marijuana, probably the mildest illegal drug, should be made legal. They believe that there should be no penalty for buying and using small amounts of the drug. Others feel that if marijuana is made legal, more people will use the drug because it is easy to get. What do you think? Write a short paper explaining where you stand.

THEN & NOW

"**N**ever once, until I got out of prison, did I ever record, perform, or do anything any way except stoned." So says David Crosby in his autobiography *Long Time Gone*. One of the biggest rock stars of the era, Crosby was a member of the Byrds and later of Crosby, Stills and Nash. "Sex, drugs, rock 'n' roll – I was in the middle of it from the beginning," he says.

Crosby was arrested several times for having drugs. He had seizures, and he suffered the addict's endless search for a high. But Crosby says that, during the time he was an addict, he never thought drugs were controlling his life.

Crosby was unable to break his addiction to cocaine and heroin until he was forced to – by being sentenced to prison. Now drug-free, Crosby is performing again. He also gives talks about drug abuse and encourages recovering addicts to remain free of drugs.

The Woodstock Music Festival, 1969. Half a million people gathered together for the three-day rock concert.

Hemlines and Hair

The London *Times* called fashion model Twiggy "the face of 1966."

She was unlike any other model the fashion world had ever seen. Models were supposed to be willowy. She was 5' 6" tall and downright skinny at 90 pounds. Thousands of women copied her short, boyish haircut and heavy eye makeup—white eyelids, black eyeliner in the crease of the lid, false eyelashes, lower lashes drawn on with an eyebrow pencil. Lesley Hornby, better known as Twiggy, took England and America by storm. The London *Times* called her "the face of 1966." Twiggy, like a lot of 1960s fashion, was something completely new.

Women's fashions took a swing—upward. Hemlines crept higher, inch by inch, as Mary Quant's miniskirt swept Europe and the United States. London's Carnaby Street was the young people's fashion capital of the world.

European designers introduced short dresses, some of them see-through with bands of fabric or sequins in certain necessary places. But the narrow miniskirts and minidresses had wide appeal. Other fashionable items: thigh-high boots, boldly printed or glittering panty hose, big chain belts, and wigs.

Fashion went wild. In America and England, guys and girls bought up old army-style uniforms. Nehru jackets with high buttoned collars were popular, and the Beatles brought on a new rage: tunic jackets with high stand-up collars.

Kids also made fashion with everyday clothes: blue jeans and T-shirts. Long used as work clothes, jeans in the mid-1960s were worn by both young men and women. Washed out, frayed, brightly embroidered, and in new shapes like bell-bottoms, jeans

were almost a uniform for the young in the late 1960s and early 1970s—and beyond.

The fashion economy was fueled by kids. By the mid-1960s, 38 million Americans were between the ages of 14 and 25. The young had money to spend, and one of the things they spent it on was clothes. Long and often shapeless "granny" dresses showed that you didn't care about fashion and being sexy. Headbands, love beads, and Indian dresses and shirts said, "I am a hippie." If you were into Eastern religions, you wore the robes that Eastern mystics wore. People tried to say through their clothing who they were. And they didn't let the fashion designers say what they should wear. They chose new styles, or no styles, or styles they created themselves.

Hair Down to There

Eventually, the styles of the young affected adult America. As more women entered the work force, for instance, some chose to wear pantsuits instead of dresses.

The biggest change, however, had to do not with fashion but with grooming: long hair and beards for men. In the mid-1960s, the Beatles shocked older

Americans with their "long" hair: it just touched their ears. Boys were expelled from school for copying the Beatles' "mop tops." But soon, mustaches, sideburns, and full beards were sprouting on the faces of rock singers, hippies, and college students.

By the 1970s, many American men, even businessmen, had caught up with the youthful style in both fashion and grooming. They began to shed their gray flannel suits for more colorful clothing and grow beards and mustaches. By the mid-1970s, businessmen often had longer hair than the Beatles had worn 10 years before. ■

Fashion went wild in the 1960s, as shown by fashion drawings of those times.

Which current fashion style or hairstyle do you really like? Which do you really hate? Write a paragraph explaining why.

The British Are Coming!

"So this is America," said the long-haired young man, watching reporters and photographers shove toward him like a tidal wave. "They all seem out of their minds."

His name was Ringo Starr. Add John Lennon, Paul McCartney, and George Harrison, and you have a rock group called the Beatles. In the early 1960s, American teenagers went out of their minds for British rock music. When the Beatles came to the United States in 1964, screaming fans met them at every airport and every concert.

"Twenty-nine hundred . . . Beatlemaniacs gave a concert early last evening at Carnegie Hall," reported the *New York Times*, "accompanied by the thumping twanging rhythms of the Beatles. . . . " Writer Tom Wolfe described the scene at a 1965 concert in San Francisco: "The whole front section of the arena becomes a writhing, seething mass of little girls waving their arms in the air . . . like a single . . . animal with a thousand waving pink tentacles. . . . Thousands of teeny bodies hurtling toward the stage . . . a solid line of cops, fighting to hurl the assault back. . . . "

American parents didn't like the Beatles being so popular with their daughters. And they didn't much like it when their sons started letting their hair grow longer and wearing "Beatle suits"—collarless jackets and pants with tight "stovepipe" legs. But the Beatles had plenty of charm and humor. They soon won over many of their critics. "How do you find America?" one reporter asked. "Turn left at Greenland" was the reply. Also, the Beatles were as clean and cute as choirboys, and their songs

The Beatles (left to right) posing for the cameras on "The Ed Sullivan Show" in 1964: Paul McCartney, George Harrison, Ringo Starr, John Lennon.

Check your local library for records or tapes by the Beatles. Some of the most famous ones are A Hard Day's Night, Rubber Soul, Sgt. Pepper's Lonely Hearts Club Band, The Beatles *(the White Album), and* Abbey Road.

Ask people of different ages what they remember about the Beatles—and how, if at all, the group and its songs were important to them. Then write a report about their answers.

THEN & NOW

The Beatles' music lingers on in our lives . . . on radio "all Beatles" weekends . . . as background music in movies about the 1960s . . . even as the piped-in background music in grocery stores. For a generation of Americans now in their 40s, the music still brings back fond memories. To them, the songs of the Beatles will always be the sound of their youth.

Newspaper columnist Bob Greene remembers "the days when a new Beatles record would be released every six weeks or so; each one was like a gift, a new chorus for the sound track of our lives." And, he adds, he prefers to think not of the sad ending of Beatle John Lennon's life (he was murdered in 1980), but of "summer nights with 'Sgt. Pepper' coming out of the car radio, and life stretching out ahead like the most perfect and level two-lane highway ever built."

To those who heard the Beatles' songs when they first came out, such feelings are still alive.

The Beatles (left to right) in about 1968: George, Paul, John, Ringo. Gone is the clean-cut "choirboy" look; in its place is the hippie look.

had catchy tunes and pleasant lyrics. (Later, such Beatles albums as 1967's *Sgt. Pepper's Lonely Hearts Club Band* and 1968's *The Beatles,* called the White Album, would explore more serious subjects.)

The Beatles were followed by other popular British rock groups—the Rolling Stones, the Animals, the Kinks, the Who, and others. The press called it a "British invasion." But this invasion had American roots. In the 1950s, America had sent the sounds of rock 'n' roll to England. British teenagers went crazy for stars like Fats Domino, Elvis Presley, Chuck Berry, and Buddy Holly. In the 1960s, the British returned the favor. They added a British flavor to American rock—and sent their brand of rock back to the United States. ■

That Sweet Soul Music

During the 1960s, different styles of black American music – gospel songs from the churches, blues from the nightclubs and bars – came together in a new style that people called "soul." But what *was* soul?

Singer Aretha Franklin, whose style earned her the title "Queen of Soul," called soul music a marriage of heaven and hell. "How do you sing?" an interviewer once asked her. "Religiously," said Aretha, who started her performing career singing in her father's church.

Like gospel songs, soul music was full of feeling. With the right song, a soul performer could put listeners into a nearly hysterical state. Soul singers such as "Soul Brother Number One" James Brown, Isaac Hayes, Otis Redding, and "Wicked" Wilson Pickett

took this "church" tradition and brought it into the world – singing songs about the love (and the troubles) between men and women.

Motown: "The Sound of Young America"

Young America snapped its fingers and moved its feet to another 1960s sound. The "Motown Sound" had a huge impact on popular music that is still felt today. Many of the singers that Motown Records produced are legends: Stevie Wonder, Diana Ross and the Supremes, the Temptations, Smokey Robinson and the Miracles, Gladys Knight and the Pips, Marvin Gaye, the Jackson Five, the Four Tops, and Martha and the Vandellas, to name the most famous.

Just what was the Motown Sound?

"Queen of Soul" Aretha Franklin, as she looked in the 1960s.

Berry Gordy, Jr., founder of Motown Records, once described it as "a combination of rats, roaches, love, and guts." A Motown staffer said it was made of "chitlins, grits, and the ghetto." Actually, it was a blend of rhythm and blues and soul, with a dash of gospel, that appealed to a wide audience. Motown was the only record company that was identified more by its *sound* than by its singers. Recording stars such as the Beatles and the Rolling Stones credited Motown for influencing their music.

Hitsville, U.S.A.

Gordy, a one-time amateur boxer and auto-assembly-line worker, founded the company in 1959 on an $800 family loan. He named it "Motown," short for Detroit's nickname, "Motor Town." The recording studio was located in a two-story house on Grand Boulevard in Detroit and was dubbed "Hitsville, U.S.A." Hitsville turned out to be a well-chosen name. From its first million-seller, "Shop Around," by the Miracles in 1961, Motown went on to produce more hits than any other record company of its size. Between 1964 and 1965, the Supremes, one of its best known acts, racked up five number-one hits in a row to become the most successful female group in pop-music history.

The Later Years

In the early 1970s, Motown Records moved to California, to expand into television and movies. By then it had become the largest and wealthiest black-owned business in America. By the late 1970s, most of its major stars had left the label and its influence on popular music had begun to decline.

In 1988, Gordy sold the label to MCA Records for more than $60 million. He retained ownership of the music-publishing arm of the company.

In the mid-1980s, the old Hitsville recording studios on Grand Boulevard in Detroit were converted into a museum. Today you can see the place that made music history. You can hear, piped in through speakers, the driving rhythms of the Fender bass, the shaking tambourines, the wail of the sax, and the throbbing drums that all worked together to create the Motown Sound, the sound that won the hearts of young America. ■

Two of Motown's finest: the Temptations (left) and Smokey Robinson (right).

Have you ever been deeply moved by a live performance of a piece of music? Write a few sentences about a time when music affected you strongly.

New Stars on Television

Johnny Carson (right) with sidekick Ed McMahon on the "Tonight" show during the 1960s.

Is TV a "vast wasteland"? That's what Federal Communications Commission chairman Newton Minow said in 1961. He wasn't alone. Critics said television wasn't as exciting and creative as in the "golden age" of the early 1950s. But more people were watching more hours of TV than ever before.

There were bright spots: 1961's "The Dick Van Dyke Show" gave a new sparkle to the tired old sitcom format. Dick Van Dyke played Rob Petrie, a TV comedy writer. Mary Tyler Moore played his wife, Laura, an ex-dancer. Their friends on the show were people in the entertainment business. It was the right show for the Kennedy years, when Americans felt young and hip.

In 1962, a young comic named Johnny Carson took over the "Tonight" show after host Jack Paar fought with NBC censors. After a shaky start, Carson made the late-night talk show the place to be on TV—and he stayed on top until he turned over the show to Jay Leno in 1992.

As the 1960s went on, TV programmers made room for some shows that were different. "That Was the Week That Was" had a news program format—but poked fun at the week's "real" news. "The Smothers Brothers Comedy Hour" starred Tom and Dick Smothers, a comedy/folksinging team. The show gave them a chance to try their offbeat humor on a big audience. Their political jokes came at a time when antiwar feeling was growing. But CBS, worried about offending viewers who supported the war, canceled the show.

The most successful show to mix comedy and political humor was "Rowan & Martin's Laugh-In." Starting in 1967, the show was a collection of "bits": one-line jokes, repeated "sight gags" (visual humor), songs, and short skits. One joke followed another at high speed. While some of the jokes were old, the look of the show was very 1960s. Sexy women with funny sayings painted on their bodies danced in bathing suits or miniskirts. (Actress Goldie Hawn began her career as a "Laugh-In" "girl.") The political humor was all in fun. The politicians who were the show's favorite targets (such as Richard Nixon and Barry Goldwater) sometimes appeared briefly on the show.

Spies and Spacemen

The tension between the United States and the Soviet Union was background for the spy shows "I Spy" and "The Man from U.N.C.L.E." As one of a pair of U.S. secret agents on "I Spy," comedian Bill Cosby was the first black American to have an ongoing starring dramatic role on television. U.N.C.L.E. (United Network Command for Law Enforcement) was a fictional spy organization that battled THRUSH—an evil organization of villains from around the world. The more popular of the two U.N.C.L.E. agents was Illya Kuryakin, played by Scottish actor David McCallum. In the show's story line, Kuryakin was a Russian who had defected to the United States. McCallum's Beatle haircut and good looks made "The Man from U.N.C.L.E." especially popular with young women.

The outer-space series "Star Trek" was a more serious show. Set in the 23rd century, it showed people of many races—and both sexes—working together in harmony. "Here was a future it did not hurt to imagine," remembers one early fan. "Here was a constructive tomorrow for mankind, emphasizing exploration and expansion."

Realistic Comedies

In the early 1970s, real-world problems began to show up in TV comedies like "M*A*S*H" and "All in the Family." "M*A*S*H" was an antiwar comedy about an army medical team serving in the Korean War of the 1950s. But it seemed really to be about the war in Vietnam. The team's doctors and nurses tried to understand the Asian culture around them—and tried to keep their sanity in what seemed to be a meaningless war.

Scenes from popular TV shows "Laugh-In" (left), "Star Trek" (center), "I Spy" (bottom right), and "M*A*S*H" (top).

Few TV producers thought "All in the Family" would do well when it started in 1971. But Norman Lear, who created it, says that the TV networks learned something from the show's popularity: "[They] learned that America was far more grown-up than they had thought."

"All in the Family" focused on the Bunkers—Archie and Edith—and their daughter and son-in-law, who lived with them. Shows about families were

In a scene from "All in the Family" (above), Archie (right) is having one of his many arguments with Michael (left), whom Archie called "Meathead." The cast of "Sesame Street" (below) in the mid-1970s.

Big Bird Comes in for a Landing

Writers have called it "the longest street in the world." It's "Sesame Street," the TV street where several generations of children around the world have learned the ABCs, the 1-2-3s, and plenty more. In Mexico, "Sesame Street" is called "Plaza Sesamo." In France, it's "Rue Sesame"; in the Philippines, "Sesame"; in Arab nations, "Iftah Ya Simsim"; and in Israel, "Rechov Sumsum."

"Sesame Street" and its characters—Big Bird, Kermit the Frog, Oscar the Grouch, Bert and Ernie, and the Cookie Monster—were created in the late 1960s to help children get ready to do well in school. To get children interested in learning, the show used many of the techniques of commercials—cartoons, musical jingles, a fast pace.

Along the way, "Sesame Street" taught lessons about people too. The cast included white, African-American, Hispanic, and Asian actors. An elderly actor was a key character—and when the actor died, the show dealt gently with the subject of death. In recent years, "Sesame Street" has let children get to know characters who are physically and mentally challenged.

nothing new. What made this family-based show different was Archie. Archie was a bigot—he believed and repeated insulting ideas about minority groups. His comments about blacks, Hispanics, Jews, Asians, the elderly, homosexuals, feminists, students, and many other groups were always ignorant and mean. They made people squirm. But many Americans really did talk like Archie Bunker.

"All in the Family" did not support bigotry. Real-life bigots couldn't enjoy Archie Bunker, because he was so obviously a fool. He usually paid in some way for his prejudice. Also, his hip son-in-law, Michael, always pointed out the stupidity of Archie's beliefs. The arguments between the two characters were often the highlight of the show. And Archie, for all his wrong ideas, was lovable. He meant well, and he truly cared about his family. "All in the Family" helped Americans laugh at their own ignorance—ignorance that they hoped they had left behind. ■

Which of the 1960s and early 1970s television shows have you seen as reruns? Which would you like to see? In your opinion, are today's television shows better or worse than in the past?

Newton Minow called television "a vast wasteland." What do you think he meant by this? Do you agree with Minow's comparison? How could television be better than it is?

American soldiers fighting in Vietnam during the height of the war, February 1968. Television coverage turned many Americans against the war.

Television and the News

News reports were part of TV almost from the beginning. But by the 1960s, television was not just reporting the news; it was affecting it. TV news coverage of the Kennedy-Nixon debates may have given John Kennedy the edge he needed to win the 1960 presidential election. And when JFK was assassinated in 1963, TV's around-the-clock coverage of events helped Americans mourn together—and look ahead.

The nightly reports from Vietnam brought the horror of war into Americans' living rooms—and turned many Americans against the war. It wasn't just the war scenes; it was also the reporters. For example, Walter Cronkite, the anchorman for CBS News, made a trip to Vietnam in 1968. After he returned, Cronkite talked openly about his feeling that the United States should get out of the war. He learned later that President Lyndon Johnson also believed in TV's ability to influence people. Worried about Americans' attitudes toward the war, Johnson said, "Well, if I've lost Cronkite, I've lost middle America."

Radical Words

A scene from *Hair*, the popular Broadway hippie musical.

A Broadway musical called *Hair*, about barefoot, long-haired hippies? And *Oh! Calcutta!,* a musical with a naked cast that pretended to have sex onstage? New voices were making themselves heard in the American theater and literature of the 1960s – the "Age of Aquarius." To many Americans, the ideas of these new writers and composers were shocking.

Some of the best writers of the 1960s centered their work around the hot social issues of the day. Joseph Heller's novel *Catch-22* is a dark, comic look at the horrors of war. It captured the imagination of young Americans who were protesting to stop the war in Vietnam. So did Kurt Vonnegut's popular antiwar novel *Slaughterhouse-Five*.

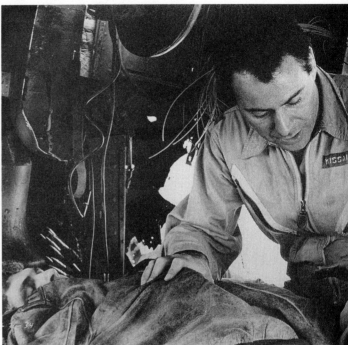

African-American writer Eldridge Cleaver, a member of the Black Panthers, made the bestseller list in 1968 with a fiery collection of essays, *Soul on Ice*. Cleaver criticized America's treatment of blacks and called for "total liberty for blacks or total destruction of America."

In theater, black playwrights like Leroi Jones (Imamu Amiri Baraka), Ed Bullins, and Adrienne Kennedy wrote angry plays about racism. Many of these plays were emotional experiences for the audiences. In Baraka's biting play *Dutchman*, a white woman named Lula comes on to a black man named Clay. When he tries to accept her offer, she lashes out at him. The play dramatizes the uneasy relationship between blacks and whites during the 1960s.

Bullins's play *It Bees Dat Way* forces the audience to take part in the play. Black actors roam among the white members of the audience. They push, shove, and insult them. In the end, the play isn't on stage at all—it's in the reactions of audience members, both black and white, to this racial situation.

Kennedy's *Funnyhouse of a Negro* tells the haunting story of Sarah, a black woman who cannot accept her African roots. Taught by white society to believe that blacks are evil, Sarah kills herself.

The bitter messages of these plays brought new audiences to the American theater—and a renewed interest in black drama. ∎

Nudity on stage? Sex acted out on stage? Plays in which the actors insult the audience? Theater became daring in the 1960s and 1970s. What do you think of these kinds of plays? Would you go to see them?

The U.S. Constitution guarantees "freedom of speech." Do you believe plays like these should be protected by the Constitution's guarantee?

"I Am the Greatest"

Muhammad Ali (right) sending heavyweight champion George Foreman to the canvas during their 1974 "Rumble in the Jungle" in Zaire.

"Float like a butterfly. Sting like a bee. Rumble, young man, rumble." This was the battle cry of young Cassius Clay, later known as Muhammad Ali. During much of the 1960s and 1970s, Ali was the top boxer in the world. He called himself the greatest fighter who ever lived, a claim many boxing fans would agree with. Ali was the first and only boxer to win the heavyweight championship three separate times.

When Cassius Clay was 18 years old, he won a gold medal in the 1960 Olympics in Rome, Italy. Four years later, he beat Sonny Liston to win his first world heavyweight championship. Most boxing experts had predicted Liston would win easily. After the match, Clay shouted to reporters, "I told you I was gonna get Liston and I got him. . . . I proved all of you wrong. I shook up the world! Tell me who is The Greatest!"

Because of his bragging, many Americans did not like Clay. But they had to admit he was quite a boxer. From 1964 through 1967, he defended his title nine times.

He also brought a different style to heavyweight boxing. Heavyweights had usually been slow, even clumsy, but very strong. Clay had a good punch, and he proved he could take the best an opponent could give. But he brought to boxing a "dancing" style that was new. He described this style in his autobiography: "I would be as fast as a lightweight, circle, dance, shuffle, hit and move, zip-zip-pop-pop, hit and move back and dance again and make an art out of [boxing]."

During the early and mid-1960s, Cassius Clay underwent a personal change. Like a number of African-Americans of that time, he had become interested in the Black Muslim religion. In 1964, he joined the Nation of Islam and changed his name to Muhammad Ali.

In 1967, Ali was drafted by the U.S. Army. But he refused to serve, because of his religious beliefs. His refusal shocked many Americans. To people protesting the Vietnam War, he was a hero. But to others, he was simply a "draft dodger."

Soon after, Ali was arrested and sentenced to five years in prison for refusing to go into the army. As a result of the conviction, the World Boxing Association (WBA) stripped him of his heavyweight title. After a four-year court battle, the Supreme Court reversed the sentence. Ali never went to prison. But he did lose four years as a boxer – a big part of any pro athlete's short career.

By 1971, the time was right for him to make a comeback. Many Americans had turned against the war in Vietnam. Ali's refusal to serve no longer seemed so bad to them. Powerful Joe Frazier was heavyweight champion at that time. Ali fought him on March 8, 1971. Neither fighter could "knock out" the other – so the fight was decided by the boxing judges. They ruled that Frazier was still champion.

Ali was still a magnificent fighter. But most experts thought he had slowed down a bit. He continued to fight, hoping for another chance at the title. At times, it seemed he would not get it. For example, in 1973, he was defeated by Ken Norton, who broke Ali's jaw. Six months later, however, Ali defeated Norton. And in 1974, Ali regained the world championship when he defeated George Foreman in Zaire, Africa.

Foreman entered the fight with a perfect 40–0 record, including 37 knockouts. Ali, six years older than

Muhammad Ali (left) having his headgear removed after sparring. His trainer (right) wears Ali's famous motto on his shirt.

Muhammad Ali protesting against the Vietnam War in 1967, shortly after having been convicted of draft evasion.

Ali the Poet

Muhammad Ali loved to write rhymes that made fun of his opponents. In verse, he would predict the round in which he would knock them out. "They all must fall / In the round I call," he sang.

He wrote his life story in verse:
It all started twenty years
    past,
The Greatest of them all was
    born at last.
The very first words from his
    Louisville lips
"I'm pretty as a picture and
    there's no one I can't
    whip."
Then he said in a voice that
    sounded rough
"I'm as strong as an ox
    And twice as tough."

The name of this Champ,
    I might as well say,
No other than The Greatest,
    Cassius Clay.

Before fighting Joe Frazier, Ali sang:
I'm gonna come out smokin',
    And I won't be jokin'.
I'm gonna be a peckin' and a
    pokin',
Pouring water on his
    smokin'.
It might shock you and amaze
    ya,
But I'm gonna destroy Joe
    Frazier!

"They all must fall/ In the round I call."

Foreman, was the underdog. Ali started the fight slowly, losing the early rounds. But Foreman became tired, and Ali knocked him down in the eighth round to become world heavyweight champion once again.

"I take nothing away from George," said Muhammad Ali after the fight. "He can still beat any man in the world. Except me."

Ali successfully defended the title 10 times; then he lost it to Leon Spinks in February 1978. But he regained it from Spinks in September of the same year. The fight was one for the record books. It was the third time Ali had taken the world championship away from another titleholder. ∎

Muhammad Ali was stripped of his heavyweight boxing title because he refused to enter the U.S. Army. Do you think this was fair? If an athlete is found guilty of breaking a law, should he or she still be allowed to compete?

Few people had lukewarm feelings about Muhammad Ali. Most either loved him or hated him. Ask five or six people who followed Ali's career to describe him in one word. Compare the results.

FOOTBALL MANIA

For almost 40 years, the National Football League (NFL) had been the United States' only professional football league. But in 1960, the NFL had competition. The American Football League (AFL) was formed. By the end of the 1960s, new competition would make pro football much more popular.

At first, many people laughed at the AFL. Its teams usually did not make money. And most of its players were not as good as those in the NFL.

But from the start, the AFL had a plan to build a powerful league. It offered big money to top players graduating from college. Some young players signed contracts with teams from both the AFL and the NFL, then played for the team that offered the most money. In one famous case, Billy Cannon, the top college player in 1959, signed a contract with the Los Angeles Rams of the NFL. "I've always wanted to play for the Rams," said Cannon. But then, a few weeks later, Cannon signed with the Houston Oilers of the AFL. The Rams and the Oilers went to court. The court ruled in favor of the AFL, and the Oilers got Cannon.

By the mid-1960s, the two leagues realized that their rivalry over players had become costly. It had driven up players' salaries and resulted in some expensive court fights. So the leagues took action. In 1967, the NFL agreed to play games against the AFL teams. The first game matched the champion of each league. The NFL's Green Bay Packers beat the AFL's Kansas City Chiefs 35–10. After the 1969 season, the two leagues became one. The AFL became the American Football Conference (AFC) of the new National Football League. The old NFL became the National Football Conference (NFC) of the new league.

This new arrangement brought in

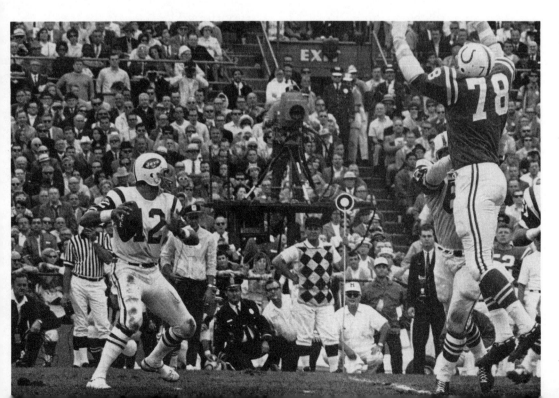

The Super Bowl brought new excitement to pro football in the 1960s. Here, New York Jets quarterback Joe Namath looks for a receiver in the 1969 Super Bowl.

The Green Bay Packers carrying coach Vince Lombardi off the field after winning the NFL championship in 1966. One year later, Lombardi and the Packers would win the first Super Bowl.

new fans. As for the championship game, which soon became known as the Super Bowl, it was soon accepted by America's fans as the *true* championship. Football had created a championship game to compare with baseball's World Series. ■

THEN & NOW

On January 28, 1990, the hottest ticket in New Orleans was for Super Bowl XXIV. The game was between the San Francisco 49ers and the Denver Broncos. Sports fans across the country wanted to be a part of the lavish parties and wild parades that made the game more like a week-long celebration. "There may have been only one game in town, but there definitely was more than one party," a reporter wrote. The media and fans occupied just about every hotel room available. More than 2,000 seats were reserved for reporters. Most tickets for the game cost $100 or more.

Just 23 years earlier, the first AFL-NFL championship had received much less publicity. The NFL's Green Bay Packers had played the AFL's Kansas City Chiefs. The event had none of the flash and fame of later Super Bowls. Even though tickets cost $12 or less, more than one-third of the seats in the Los Angeles Memorial County Stadium remained empty. Television commercial time had cost $85,000 for one minute. But in Super Bowl XXIV, just 30 seconds cost $700,000.

Leader of the Pack

"Winning isn't everything. It's the only thing," said Vince Lombardi, the coach of the NFL's Green Bay Packers from 1959 to 1967. Lombardi's Packers won five NFL championships and the first two Super Bowls.

"This is a violent sport. To play in this league, you've got to be tough—physically tough and mentally tough," said Lombardi. He expected his players to play hard even when injured.

Lombardi died of cancer in 1970, but he is not forgotten. Since 1971, the team that wins the Super Bowl has received the Vince Lombardi Trophy.

Sports Superstars

In the 1960s and early 1970s, sports in the United States had more than its share of larger-than-life figures. Outstanding athletes dominated all sports and set impressive records. Here's a scorecard of some of the headline makers of the not-too-distant past—introduced by their colorful nicknames.

"The Home Run King"

"Some guys love the life of a celebrity... but all it brought me was headaches," said baseball player Roger Maris. In 1961, Maris hit 61 home runs. Babe Ruth's record of 60 homers in one season had stood for 34 years.

Maris broke Ruth's record in the last game of the baseball season. For weeks, reporters had been hounding Maris, waiting for him to break the record. They followed him to his locker before games started and waited for him when games ended.

Fans also bothered Maris. While some adored him, others were angry with him for challenging the record of the beloved Babe. For the same reason, he even received hate mail.

Maris was a quiet man who liked his privacy. He did not enjoy his newfound fame. "It would have been a helluva lot more fun if I had never hit those 61 home runs," he said. But baseball would have been deprived of its most famous record.

"Hammerin' Hank"

On the night of April 8, 1974, Henry (Hank) Aaron stood at home plate with bat in hand. He was about to make baseball history by breaking Babe Ruth's career record of 714 home runs.

The place was Atlanta–Fulton County Stadium. Aaron swung and hit a line drive home run over the left-field fence—the 715th of his career.

The usually unemotional Aaron burst into tears as he circled the bases and reached home plate. His teammates lined up to congratulate him. He hugged his mother.

"I remember my mother out there," Aaron said. "And she was hugging me. That's what I'll remember more than anything about that home run."

By the end of his career, Aaron had 755 homers—41 more than Babe Ruth.

"The Man with the Golden Arm"

One of baseball's best pitchers almost quit the game early in his career. Sandy Koufax, a left-handed pitcher for the Dodgers, played poorly for the first half of his 12-year career. Now he is considered one of the greatest pitchers of all time.

During his first six years in the majors, Koufax won only 36 games and lost 40—a so-so record. Finally, in his seventh season, Koufax gained control of his pitching. His blazing fastball set up his sharp-breaking curve.

"They [batters] just stopped hitting him," said his manager, Walter Alston. "And it happened in one year."

Koufax became a winning pitcher. During his next five seasons, 1962–1966, he won 111 games and lost 34. It was an incredible record. But Koufax suffered from arthritis in his pitching arm. After every game, he

Hank Aaron watches his 715th home run fly out of the park on April 8, 1974, breaking Babe Ruth's career home run record.

took painkilling pills and put his elbow in ice-cold water to ease the swelling. After the 1966 season, doctors told him that he must stop pitching or risk arm problems for the rest of his life. Koufax's career ended when he was only 30 years old.

Between 1962 and 1966, Sandy Koufax won 111 games and lost only 34.

"The Stilt"

Standing 7' 2" and weighing 300 pounds, Wilt Chamberlain was a major force on the basketball court. Players did anything they could to stop him from scoring. During a college championship game, players from the University of North Carolina would not let him shoot the ball. "We just surrounded Wilt," said the North Carolina coach. "Whenever he got the ball, we were all over him." It worked. Wilt's team, the University of Kansas, lost the game.

Wilt was an even more dominant player in professional basketball. On March 2, 1962, Chamberlain scored 100 points in a single game. No other player has even come close to scoring that many points. Chamberlain's team, the Philadelphia Warriors (now the 76ers), won that game 169–147 over the New York Knicks. "The Knicks started to do anything they could to prevent me from scoring 100 points," said Chamberlain. That made him play even harder.

Chamberlain once jokingly complained, "Nobody roots for Goliath." But Wilt the Stilt was one giant whom millions cheered.

"The Golden Bear"

The greatest golfer of all time started playing because of his father's injury. When Jack Nicklaus was 10 years old, his father was playing lots of golf to strengthen an injured ankle. He began taking Jack with him to the golf course. The young Nicklaus soon showed a remarkable talent for golf.

Nicklaus practiced for many hours to improve his game. His coach was impressed by his dedication. "No one ever worked harder at golf than Nicklaus during his teens and early twenties," he said. "At the age of 10, in his first year of golf, Jack must have averaged at least 300 practice shots and

at least 18 holes of play daily."

It paid off. Nicklaus was U.S. Amateur champion in 1959 and again in 1961. The next year, at the age of 22, Nicklaus won the U.S. Open title. During the 1960s and 1970s, he won all the major championships in his sport. By the 1970s, he was recognized as golf's greatest player.

"The Magician"

It seemed that every time hockey player Bobby Orr stepped onto the ice, he performed "magic." His coach called him "a star from the moment they played the National Anthem in his first National Hockey League [NHL] game." That was in 1966. Orr was then 18 years old.

Bobby Orr played defense for the Boston Bruins. His job was to stop other players from scoring goals. But Orr did much more. He was a superb defender—but he also used his lightning-quick speed to race past opponents and score goals. Suddenly, a defensive player was one of the NHL leaders in scoring. It was like a pitcher leading a baseball league in hitting home runs.

Bobby Orr's jersey hangs from the ceiling of Boston Garden—a tribute to one of Boston's greatest athletes.

"Broadway Joe"

When the New York Jets football team paid rookie quarterback Joe Namath a record $427,000, they were investing in their future. "When Joe Namath walks into a room, you know he's there. When another rookie walks in, he's just another nice-looking kid. Namath's like Babe Ruth or Lou Gehrig," said Jets president Sonny Werblin.

Even before joining the Jets, Namath had been a great athlete. In high school, he had played football, basketball, and baseball. After graduation, baseball's Baltimore Orioles offered him $20,000 to play. Instead, Namath went to the University of Alabama to play football.

Later, as a professional football player, Namath brought the American Football League its most important victory up to that point. The AFL had never beaten the NFL in the Super Bowl. In 1969, the Jets made it to the Super Bowl. "We'll win. I guarantee it," Namath said before the game. The Jets

Wilt Chamberlain (above left) scored 100 points in a single game. Joe Namath (above right) "guaranteed" that his New York Jets would beat the favored Baltimore Colts in Super Bowl III. They did.

defeated the Baltimore Colts 16–7.

Namath's off-the-field lifestyle was as famous as his football career. He loved staying out late, going to nightclubs, and having a good time. "I've always had a happy attitude my whole life," Namath once said. Namath also was a rebel, known for making his own rules and questioning authority. For this reason, he became a hero to rebellious young people. ∎

Which of the 1960s sports heroes interests you most? Look for more information about them in your local library. Hank Aaron's 1991 autobiography, I Had a Hammer, *may be of special interest. In it, Aaron talks about his baseball career and the racial prejudice he had to overcome.*

Billie Jean King returns the ball to 55-year-old Bobby Riggs, who had challenged her to the match. Millions of TV viewers watched King defeat Riggs.

King of the Court

Men and women rarely compete against one another in professional sports. But in 1973, tennis player Bobby Riggs challenged female star Billie Jean King to a tennis match.

Riggs said that female players could not win matches against male players. He also said that despite his age of 55, he could beat the best female athletes.

Riggs's statements angered King. She was the top female tennis player in the world, having won the U.S. Open in 1971 and 1972 and Wimbledon in 1972 and 1973.

She was also a feminist. She thought Riggs's remarks hurt women's professional tennis. So she agreed to play Riggs to prove him wrong.

More than 30,000 people bought tickets for the historic match, which was held at the Astrodome in Houston on September 20, 1973. And more than 50 million people in 36 nations saw it on television. It was the largest audience ever to watch a tennis match.

King beat Riggs 6–4, 6–3, 6–3.

"She was too good. . . . It was over too quickly," said Riggs.

Billie Jean King had saved women's tennis from embarrassment. But Bobby Riggs wasn't crying. He got a nice paycheck even though he lost. He also got tons of publicity – which may be what he was really after.

Olympic Gold— and Murder

The 1964 Olympics in Tokyo, Japan, were the first ever held in Asia. Japan opened its heart to the Olympians. "The entire nation, from newsboy to industrial tycoon, adopted the Games," said the president of the International Olympic Committee.

American athletes pleased the crowds back home by setting many world records. Bill Bradley led the U.S. men's basketball team to its sixth straight gold medal. A little-known American runner, Billy Mills, won the 10,000-meter run. He ran past world record holders from Australia, Great Britain, the USSR, and New Zealand.

Politics Takes Over

Political trouble stole the show at the 1968 Olympic Games, which were held in Mexico City. Several weeks before the Olympics, University of Mexico students marched in support of the poor. Thirty-three students were killed by Mexican police.

Then, black athletes threatened to boycott the Olympics. They wanted to show the world that African-Americans were treated unfairly in America. Although black athletes took part in the games, two African-American medal winners bowed their heads and raised black-gloved fists in the air while America's national anthem was being played. The president of the International Olympic Committee said the athletes went against "the basic standards of good manners and sportsmanship" and sent them home.

U.S. Olympic medalists Tommie Smith (center) and John Carlos (right) giving the Black Power salute during the 1968 Olympics.

Controversy and Triumph

The United States also had its problems at the 1972 games in Munich, Germany. Because of a scheduling error, two of the best American runners never arrived at their race. And in the 1,500 meters, American Jim Ryun, the world record holder, was knocked to the ground and lost.

But the worst luck came at the end of the basketball championship game against the Soviet Union. The Americans thought that time had run out while they were ahead 50–49. But the Russians were given three extra seconds by the referees. The Russians scored a basket to win 51–50.

Despite these losses, America had reason to celebrate. America's best swimmer in the 1972 Olympics won a remarkable seven gold medals. Mark Spitz entered four individual events and three relays. In each race, he set or helped set a new world record.

Massacre at Munich

The glow of good feeling created by Spitz was lost, however, in the pain of an incredible tragedy. The 1972 Olympic Games in Munich will be remembered for the murders of 11 Israeli athletes. On September 5, eight members of the Black September, a Palestinian terrorist group, entered the Israeli team's sleeping quarters and began shooting.

Two Israelis were killed instantly, and nine were kidnapped.

The terrorists took the nine Israelis to an airport so that they could be flown to an Arab country. Several nations tried to talk to the terrorists, but they refused to listen.

Police tried to rescue the Israelis. Finally, there was a bloody gun battle between terrorists and police at the airport. All of the Israeli hostages died. Many people thought the police had mishandled the situation. Some said

American runner Jim Ryun (above) falls during a heat of the 1,500 meters at the 1972 Olympics. Ryun, the world record holder, finished next to last. Swimmer Mark Spitz (right) holds five of the seven gold medals he won at the 1972 games.

RY, SEPTEMBER 6, 1972

ISRAELIS ON OLYMPIC TEAM KILLED WITH 4 ARAB CAPTORS AS POLICE FIGHT BAND THAT DISRUPTED MUNICH GAMES

A 23-HOUR DRAMA

MRS. MEIR SPEAKS

are Slain in

there were not enough police at the airport shootout. But German officials defended their plan.

The next day, a service was held for the athletes who had died. Some countries wanted the games to end, but Olympics chairman Avery Brundage ordered the games to continue. Some countries sent their athletes home anyway. But none of what happened at the reopened games seemed to matter as much as before the murders. ■

The Olympics are supposed to be separate from politics. But often they are not.

• Should the athletes who gave the Black Power salute have been sent home from the 1968 games? Do athletes have the right to express their opinions in ways such as this?

• Should the 1972 Olympics have been called off after the murders of the Israeli athletes? Why or why not?

A masked Black September terrorist (top) stands on the balcony of the Israeli Olympic team's headquarters in Munich. An Olympic official (bottom) tries to talk with one of the terrorists.

The War on Poverty

It came out in 1962. It was a small book, not even 200 pages long. Yet it influenced two presidents, John F. Kennedy and Lyndon B. Johnson. It also helped change the lives of millions of Americans.

The Other America

Michael Harrington's book *The Other America* described the United States as two nations. One nation was a rich society. It contained about 150 million people with the highest standard of living the world had ever known. The other nation was "underdeveloped." It contained about 40 million people who were living in poverty.

What did living in poverty mean during the early 1960s? It meant that a city family of four had only about $3,000 a year to spend. That amount was less than half of what a four-person family needed to live in the average American city in 1959, according to the U.S. Bureau of Labor Statistics. Families with only $3,000 a year to spend were in trouble. After paying for food, rent, and clothing,

Children of a Kentucky coal-mining family on the front porch of their home in 1962.

they had little or no money left for medical care, education, transportation, or emergencies.

Who lived in poverty? There were four main groups, some of which overlapped: people under the age of 18, people over the age of 65, members of minority groups, and the "working poor" – people without the skills needed to hold well-paying jobs.

People living in poverty had something in common besides their lack of money. They had little or no hope for the future. Most of their parents and grandparents had also been poor. Poverty had been handed down from one generation to the next. The poor saw no way out.

The War Begins

President Kennedy read Harrington's book. He planned to push for new laws to fight poverty. But his plan was cut short. He was assassinated before he could send his programs to Congress.

Lyndon B. Johnson, who succeeded Kennedy as president, was even more determined to end poverty. Just a little over two months after he took office, he delivered a message to Congress:

This administration today, here and now, declares unconditional war on poverty in America, and I urge this Congress and all Americans to join with me in that effort.

It will not be a short or easy struggle – no single weapon or strategy will suffice [be enough] – but we shall not rest until that war is won.

Results

Between 1963 and 1969, Johnson pushed more than 200 laws through Congress. They included programs that touched on many aspects of American life, including the following:

• *Education*: The Head Start program created preschool classes for children from poor families. The classes taught

Poverty had been handed down from one generation to the next. The poor saw no way out.

Members of the Poor People's Campaign gather at the Lincoln Memorial, Washington, D.C., in 1968. Their "Resurrection City" (bottom), a makeshift camp, dramatized the problems of the poor.

the children skills they would need to succeed in school. The Job Corps gave employment training to high school dropouts and others.

• *Health*: The Medicare program provided hospital insurance for most people over the age of 65. It also provided low-cost medical insurance. Medicaid was put into place to help poor and disabled people pay their medical bills.

• *Housing*: The federal government built 248,000 housing units for poor people.

• *Food*: The federal government set up a food stamp program for families on welfare. These families could use the stamps to buy food. It also set up a program that gave poor children free breakfasts at school.

Did the United States win the war on poverty? Yes and no. It did reduce poverty overall. In 1964, about one in five Americans was poor. When Johnson left office in 1969, only about one in eight Americans was poor. The war on poverty was of special help to older people who were insured by Medicare and to children who took part in Head Start preschool classes.

The war on poverty did not help many adults who were unemployed or who did not have job skills. About 1.5 million people received job training. But the training did not always lead to good jobs. For one thing, the government did not set up job programs to give these people work. For another, the training often prepared them for jobs that were dying out. Many well-paying jobs disappeared as machines replaced workers. In addition, many companies had moved from central cities to the suburbs. Most poor people could not afford to travel or move to the faraway suburbs where the jobs were. Yet inner-city life often meant poverty.

After the Johnson administration's war on poverty was over, Michael Harrington summed up the results. "President Johnson had tried," he said. "But what was supposed to be a social war turned out to be a skirmish [small fight] and, in any case, poverty won." ■

In your opinion, what are the main causes of poverty today? If you were a member of Congress, what kinds of laws to reduce poverty would you vote for? How would you convince other lawmakers to vote the same way?

A Roller-Coaster Economy

"**I**s inflation a threat again?" So asked the editors of *Business Week* in August of 1965. They were not the only ones asking this question. Inflation was a serious economic problem throughout the second half of the 1960s and most of the 1970s.

Inflation occurs when prices go up quickly. As prices rise, the buying power of a dollar falls. As a result, people can buy fewer goods and services with their money. During the early 1960s, the inflation rate in the United States was about 2 percent a year – a low rate. But by 1965, the inflation rate had jumped to about 6 percent. To understand how the rising inflation rate affected consumers,

consider the following example. If you had bought $100.00 worth of products in 1960, you would have needed $102.00 in 1961 to buy the same amount. In 1962, you would have needed $104.04. In 1963, you would have needed $106.12. By 1965, you would have needed $110.41.

What had caused the rise in the inflation rate? The main reason was the Vietnam War. It was costing the United States almost $25 billion a year. But Johnson refused to raise taxes to pay for the war. With the military using a

An ad from the early 1960s shows food prices of those times. Inflation soon drove those prices up.

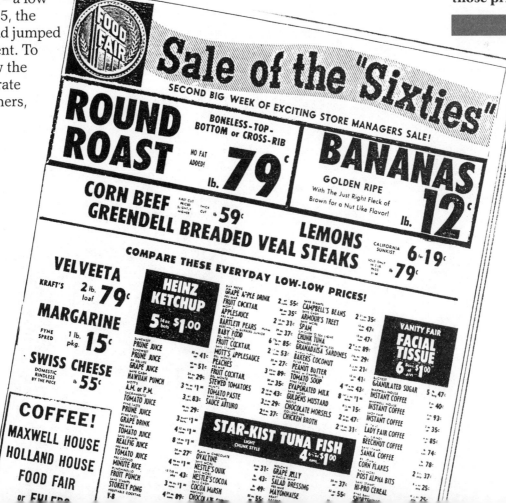

large part of what the country produced, the prices of civilian goods and services went up. By 1970, you would have needed $147.74 to buy the goods that had cost $100.00 in 1960.

Many economists believe that the way to reduce inflation is to cause a recession, or downturn in the economy. The first step is to cut spending. Lower spending means that fewer goods and services are produced. Lower production means higher unemployment. With fewer jobs available, salaries go down. When wages go down, prices do too. Lower prices mean a lower inflation rate. After a while, these economists believe, the economy will begin to grow again.

When Richard M. Nixon became president in 1969, he tried to control inflation by cutting government spending and by keeping a lid on wage and price increases. The inflation rate dipped from 6 percent in 1970 to 3.5 percent in 1972. Then, it started to rise again. It kept on rising, until it reached 11 percent in 1974. In addition, the economy did not behave the way economists said it would. Usually, production increases when inflation goes up. In the 1970s, however, production fell. As a result, the country faced a combination of inflation and recession, with almost one out of 10 workers unemployed. Economists coined a new word to describe this condition: *stagflation.* ■

Go to your public library and find a few newspapers and magazines from 1970. Use the advertisements in them to find the prices of five items, such as an automobile, a TV set, a winter coat, a movie ticket, and a pound of ground beef. Now look in today's newspapers and magazines to find the prices of the same items. How much have prices gone up? If this rate continued, what would you have to pay for the items 10 years from now?

As the graph shows, inflation means that a dollar buys less and less as prices go up.

BUYING POWER OF THE DOLLAR
1960–1975

Source: U.S. Bureau of Labor Statistics

100¢ 90¢ 80¢ 70¢ 60¢ 50¢ 40¢ 30¢ 20¢ 10¢

1960 1961 1962 1963 1964 1965 1966 1967 1968 1969 1970 1971 1972 1973 1974 1975

An Energy Crisis

SORRY OUT OF GAS!

SUPER REGULAR
Unleaded

STANDARD

Chevron

If you had gone to buy gas for your car in October 1973, you probably would have been in for a long wait in line. There was a gas shortage—the nation's first since World War II. The cause of the shortage was an Arab oil embargo. War had broken out between Israel and Egypt. Other Arab nations decided to use oil as a bargaining chip in the conflict. These nations announced that they would stop shipping—that is, *embargo*—oil to nations that supported Israel. The embargo included the United States.

The Arab oil-producing nations were Algeria, Iran, Iraq, Kuwait, Libya, Qatar, Saudi Arabia, and the United Arab Emirates. These nations, as well as five non-Arab nations, formed an organization called the Organization of Petroleum Exporting Countries (OPEC). At the same time that OPEC started the oil embargo, it tripled the price of oil.

By December of 1973, the United States was facing a major energy crisis.

During the gas shortages of the 1970s, long lines at gas stations were common.

Homes, schools, and offices were chilly as people turned thermostats down 10 degrees or more to save fuel. Some factories closed because they could not buy enough fuel to keep running. Airlines cut flights and laid off pilots and other workers. The speed limit on highways was cut to 55 mph. Lighted business signs had to be turned off after hours. Even outdoor Christmas lights were banned.

Many Americans tried to conserve. To save gas, they organized car pools to get to work. They lowered their home thermostats and started wearing sweaters indoors to keep warm. They also bought wood-burning stoves, flannel pajamas, and space heaters. Some even traded in their large cars and bought smaller cars that got more miles to the gallon of gas.

President Nixon said it was important for the United States to stop relying on other countries to supply so

Two 1973 cars (above): a "gas-guzzling" Oldsmobile Ninety Eight and a Toyota Corolla. Saudi Arabia's oil minister (right) at an OPEC conference.

Gas Guzzlers

One of the main villains in the energy crisis was gas-guzzling cars. They were the big, heavy cars that so many Americans liked to drive—cars like Cadillacs, Lincolns, and Chryslers, all made in the United States. Gas guzzlers got fewer than 10 miles per gallon of gas. In comparison, a small, light car like the Toyota Corolla from Japan got about 27 miles per gallon of gas.

SAUDI ARABIA

much of our oil. He wanted the United States to produce most of the oil it needed. But his administration did not develop a national plan to solve the energy problem. And the United States kept on importing up to 45 percent of the oil it used each year. ■

Many Americans have been trying to save energy ever since the oil embargo of 1973 and 1974. What things can you do to cut down on the amount of energy you use?

THEN & NOW

In 1991, President George Bush proposed the National Energy Strategy to Congress. He called for the United States to produce more of its own oil. Most of the new oil would come from wells in the Arctic National Wildlife Refuge in Alaska and from untouched offshore areas, like those along the coast of California.

People who were against the plan said that drilling in the Arctic National Wildlife Refuge would provide, at most, only 20 years' worth of oil. They also said that it would hurt the environment. They urged the United States to save energy instead. Among their ideas were:

• *Higher mile-per-gallon rules for cars.* Requiring cars to get 40 miles per gallon of gas would save more energy than the oil of the Alaskan coastal plain would provide. Currently, U.S. law requires new cars to get only 27.5 miles per gallon.

• *Higher gasoline taxes.* Raising taxes – and therefore prices – would force Americans to use less gasoline. The French pay about $3 per gallon. Italians pay about $4. Why should Americans, who use more oil than any other nation, pay only half as much?

• *A different transportation policy.* Encouraging railroad rather than truck freight transportation would save a great deal of energy. Rail transportation uses one-fourth the energy to move a ton of freight one mile.

• *More efficient houses.* Insulating attics and installing storm doors and windows can cut fuel needs in half. Also, a two-story town house uses 30 to 40 percent less energy than a single-family house.

• *More efficient appliances.* Designing energy-efficient goods would also save energy. For example, refrigerators would use 50 percent less electricity if their motors were on top instead of underneath and if their copper wiring were thicker.

Workers try to stay warm in a cold office. During the oil embargo, schools and businesses lowered their thermostats.

The Fight for Voting Rights

Dr. Martin Luther King, Jr., with his wife, Coretta, leads civil rights marchers on the 1965 Selma-to-Montgomery march.

"**I** can't believe this is happening in America." That's what many people said as they watched TV news reports from Selma, Alabama. The reports showed police officers—some of them on horseback—chasing and clubbing peaceful protesters.

The date was March 7, 1965. About 600 people, most of them African-Americans, were marching from Selma to Montgomery, the state capital. The marchers wanted the state government to pass laws protecting black citizens' right to vote.

Why was a march for voting rights needed at all? Didn't the Civil Rights Act of 1964 make it illegal to discriminate against people because of their race? Yes—but the Civil Rights Act was not being enforced in many parts of the South. Many southern towns and cities had made it very hard for blacks to exercise their right to vote. In many places, blacks had to pass special reading or history tests before they could register. Sometimes blacks who tried to become voters were beaten up or killed. In 1961, for example, a black man in the small town of McComb, Mississippi, was shot to death for trying to register – and the man who shot him was a state lawmaker. That's the way things were in the early 1960s. Then some brave people decided it was time for things to change.

Freedom Summer

The push for voting rights really began in the summer of 1964. Civil rights leaders wanted to register black voters throughout the South. They decided to begin in Mississippi. To help sign up voters, they asked college students, professors, ministers, and others to work as volunteers during "Freedom Summer." Many of the volunteers were young college students from the North. They opened "Freedom Schools" to teach blacks about our political system and help them learn to read.

One of the most brutal events of Freedom Summer was the murder of three civil rights workers near Philadelphia, Mississippi. Three young men – northerners Michael Schwerner and Andrew Goodman and southerner James Chaney – heard about the burning of a church in Longdale. The church was to have been the site of a Freedom School. They went to inspect the site and to talk to victims who had been beaten. The three did not return. After weeks of searching, police found their bodies in an earthen dam near Philadelphia, Mississippi. They had been shot, and Chaney, the one black man in the group, had been beaten – so badly that his skull was crushed. Although frightened by the murders, most of the volunteers stayed on.

Selma: Crossing the Bridge

The next winter, civil rights leader Dr. Martin Luther King, Jr., wanted to show the nation how much black

Americans needed a voting rights law. He chose Selma as the starting place for a nonviolent protest march. Why Selma? Although most of its citizens were black, only 3 percent of them were registered to vote. Selma's sheriff, Jim Clark, was one reason for that. Many times, Clark and his men had threatened or had beaten up blacks who tried to register.

King arrived in Selma in January of 1965 and organized several peaceful protests. They led up to the first attempt to march to Montgomery, on March 7. Marchers found policemen lining the Edmund Pettus Bridge

Civil rights workers Andrew Goodman (top left), James Chaney (bottom left), and Michael Schwerner (bottom right) were murdered in Mississippi during the "Freedom Summer" of 1964.

RIGHTS TEAM'S BURNED CAR FOUND IN MISSISSIPPI BOG;

marchers. On March 21, 1965, marchers finally crossed the bridge. Hundreds of black and white Americans walked together for the 54 miles between Selma and Montgomery. They sang "We Shall Overcome" as Alabama whites stood along the roads shouting insults.

A huge crowd of supporters met the marchers when they reached

Alabama state troopers waiting to turn back civil rights marchers during the 1965 Selma-to-Montgomery march. The marchers were making their second attempt to cross the bridge; the third time, they succeeded.

leading out of Selma. The police strategy was simple: don't let the marchers cross the bridge. On that "Black Sunday," the police attacked the marchers with tear gas, bullwhips, cattle prods, and clubs. The march was stopped.

Black Sunday outraged many Americans. President Johnson was among them. Just eight days after Black Sunday, he called a special meeting of Congress that was televised for all to see. During the meeting, he called for a law to protect blacks' right to vote. "The time for waiting is gone," he said.

But protesters' work was not over. Although the law had been proposed, Congress still had to be persuaded to pass it. More than 300 white clergy from across the nation went to Selma to join Dr. King on the next march. Police again blocked the bridge, and King had to turn his followers back. That night, a white minister from Boston who had marched with King was clubbed to death by whites from Selma.

President Johnson Steps In

As more Americans expressed their anger about what was happening in Selma, President Johnson again stepped in. He ordered the Alabama National Guard to protect the

Thurgood Marshall

Black lawyer Thurgood Marshall was a regular visitor to the U.S. Supreme Court. From the 1940s to the 1960s, Marshall argued 32 civil rights cases before the Supreme Court. He won 29 of them. It was Marshall who convinced the Court that separate schools for blacks didn't provide an education equal to that of whites. In 1954, the Court ruled that school segregation was unconstitutional. It said that public schools must be made available to students of all races.

In 1967, President Johnson appointed Thurgood Marshall to the U.S. Supreme Court – as its first African-American member. Marshall served on the court until he retired in 1991.

Montgomery on March 25. Dr. King spoke to 25,000 people in front of the Capitol. Quoting one of the marchers, he said, "Our feet are tired, but our souls are rested." Governor George Wallace refused to meet with the marchers. And that night, another marcher was killed. Michigan housewife Viola Liuzzo was a volunteer helping drive marchers back to Selma. On her last trip, she was shot to death by members of the Ku Klux Klan, a white hate group.

The Voting Rights Act

The murder of Liuzzo horrified and angered many Americans. People were already shocked by the beating of the Selma marchers. Liuzzo's murder may have been the last straw. Americans across the nation put pressure on Congress to pass the law protecting everyone's right to vote.

Congress debated for only a few weeks before passing the Voting Rights Act. President Johnson signed it on August 6, 1965. The act ended voter tests. It said that if state workers refused to sign up black voters, the federal government would send workers who would register them. It also called for poll watchers to go to southern voting places to make sure the law was being followed. In the next few years, the power of the black vote would bring many changes to both the North and South. ■

We Shall Overcome

Songs played an important part in civil rights marches. A song that marchers often sang was "We Shall Overcome." It became a symbol of the civil rights movement. The melody of this song is that of an old church hymn. The song has been sung for many years in countries around the world by people working for social change.

We shall overcome,
We shall overcome,
We shall overcome someday.
Oh, deep in my heart,
I do believe,
We shall overcome someday.

President Johnson got the song's message. He quoted the song when he first suggested a voting rights act to help overcome racial injustice. The president ended his speech by saying "We shall overcome."

Compared to the North, the South has a greater percentage of African-American elected officials in state, county, and local offices. How might the voter registration movement have contributed to the high percentage of black officials in the South?

President Johnson (left) shakes the hand of Dr. Martin Luther King, Jr., after signing the Voting Rights Act of 1965.

Voting Reforms of the 1960s

Blacks in the Deep South were not the only Americans who wanted changes in the voting laws. In 1960, citizens of Washington, D.C., could not vote for president. In some states, people had to pay money to cast a vote. And across America, citizens had to be 21 years old to vote. All of these situations would change—because of three amendments, or additions, to the U.S. Constitution.

D.C. Gets the Vote

Why couldn't the people of Washington, D.C., vote in national elections? By law, only people who live in a state can vote in national elections. And D.C.—the District of Columbia—is not a state. It was created in 1800 to be the nation's capital. Virginia and Maryland gave the land for the District of Columbia to the U.S. government.

The 23rd Amendment to the Constitution was designed to allow D.C. citizens to vote. The U.S. Congress voted yes to the amendment in 1960. Then, three-fourths of the state legislatures approved it. In 1961, the amendment became part of the Constitution. The people of D.C. got their first chance to vote for president in the 1964 election.

On November 3, 1964, residents of Washington, D.C. voted in the U.S. presidential election.

BLACK VOTER REGISTRATION IN THE SOUTH

Percentage of Voting Age Population

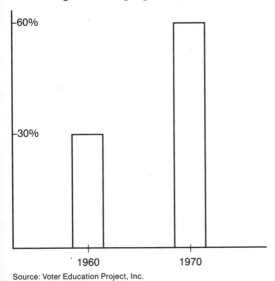

Source: Voter Education Project, Inc.

The Vietnam War had much to do with these demands. During the war, 18-year-old males could be drafted to serve in the army. Yet they could not vote until they were 21. Many young men complained that they were being sent to war by leaders they couldn't vote for—or against. Two powerful politicians, Senators Edward Kennedy and Mike Mansfield, sponsored a bill lowering the voting age to 18. They pushed Congress to pass the bill.

In 1971, Congress passed—and the states approved—the 26th Amendment. It lowered the voting age in the United States to 18. In 1972, 18- to 20-year-olds voted for U.S. president for the first time. ■

Tossing Out the Poll Tax

In America's early days, few Americans had the right to vote. Only men who owned land or belonged to certain professions, such as medicine and law, could vote. But there was a way around these requirements. Many states set up a voting fee called a *poll tax*. Nearly any male who could pay it was allowed to vote.

By the 1960s, only five states still collected poll taxes. All of these states were in the South. Many blacks could not afford to pay the tax. As a result, people felt that these states were using the poll tax as a way to keep blacks from voting.

Congress agreed that poll taxes were wrong. In 1962, it proposed the 24th Amendment, which did away with poll taxes for national elections. By 1964, the states had approved the amendment, and it became law.

Lowering the Voting Age

Like southern blacks and the people of Washington, D.C., young Americans demanded changes in the voting laws.

Do you feel that most 18-year-olds exercise their right to vote? What reasons can you offer for those who don't? Are they good reasons or not?

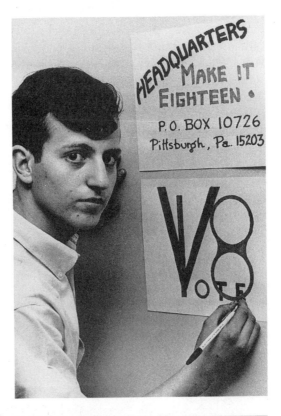

A young man working to lower the voting age to 18.

The Abortion Revolution

In 1973, seven of the Court's nine judges voted in favor of "Jane Roe." Many Americans were pleased. Many others were horrified.

In 1969, a Texas woman wanted an abortion. But abortions were illegal in Texas, and she couldn't afford to travel to a state that allowed abortions. She went to a lawyer to arrange to have her baby put up for adoption. He agreed to help her. He also put her in touch with two other lawyers, Linda Coffee and Sarah Weddington. The two lawyers wanted to challenge abortion laws like the one in Texas. The woman agreed to let them take her case to court. But she asked them not to use her real name. The lawyers called her "Jane Roe." The case was called *Roe v. Wade.* (Wade was Henry Wade, the district attorney of Dallas, where the case began.) Coffee and Weddington argued that "Roe" should have had the right to choose an abortion. The case went on for almost two years, finally ending up in the Supreme Court.

In 1973, seven of the Court's nine judges voted in favor of "Jane Roe." Many Americans were pleased. Many others were horrified.

What the Court Said

The *Roe v. Wade* decision said that states could not prevent women from having abortions during the first six months of a pregnancy. During that period, a fetus (unborn child) would have little or no chance of living if it were born. So the Court ruled that during those six months, a fetus was not protected by the law. The courts also ruled that states could choose to forbid women to have abortions during the last three months of a pregnancy, when a fetus has a good chance of surviving if born. The only exception was cases in which childbirth would endanger the mother's life.

The Issues

What was the thinking behind the Court's decision? The Court believed it was protecting the health and safety of American women. During the second half of the 1800s, when most state abortion laws were written, abortions were dangerous to the mother's health. Courts at that time had tried to protect women by making abortions illegal. By the 1960s, doctors had found ways to perform abortions safely. But women couldn't go to doctors for abortions, because the old abortion laws were still in effect. As a result, many women turned to unqualified abortionists, who might perform the operation without an anesthetic and under unsanitary conditions. Every year, hundreds of women were permanently injured by illegal abortions. Many others died.

The Court also believed it was protecting Americans' right to privacy. It ruled that this right included a woman's right to end her pregnancy. This was a private decision between a woman and her doctor, the Court said. It believed that the government should not interfere.

But what about the rights of the fetus? The lawyers who argued against "Jane Roe" said the unborn child was protected by the 14th Amendment. The amendment says that no state can "deprive any person of life" without a trial in court. But the Court held that the 14th Amendment didn't apply to the fetus. "The unborn have never been recognized in the law as persons in the whole sense," Judge Harry A. Blackmun wrote.

Two of the judges, Byron R. White and William H. Rehnquist, disagreed with the Court's ruling. White thought

it was too concerned with the mother's "convenience" and not concerned enough about the life of the unborn child. Rehnquist believed that each state should be able to make its own abortion laws.

The War over *Roe v. Wade*

Many Americans had strong feelings about the Court's decision. Pro-choice groups were pleased that women would no longer be forced to undergo dangerous, illegal abortions – or have children that they did not want. Anti-abortion groups, on the other hand, were upset. To them, abortion was murder. "No court can make something evil become something good," said Roman Catholic cardinal John Krol. "Abortion at any stage of pregnancy is evil." ■

Protesters for and against legalized abortion argue at the New Jersey State House.

What are your views on abortion? Do you think it should be legal or not? Do you think that abortions should be performed in some circumstances but not others? What experiences in your life have led you to think as you do?

THEN & NOW

Where do Americans stand on abortion nearly 20 years after *Roe v. Wade*? In several recent polls, a majority say they wouldn't want to go back to the days when all abortions were illegal. But many people want to place some restrictions on abortions.

Some members of today's Supreme Court seem to support overturning *Roe v. Wade*. In 1989, the Court issued a new decision – *Webster v. Reproductive Health Services*. It upheld some antiabortion laws in the state of Missouri that limit women's right to get abortions as outlined in the *Roe v. Wade* decision. In 1991, the Court issued another new decision – *Rust v. Sullivan*. It upheld a ruling that said health clinics receiving money from the federal government are not allowed to provide clients with information about abortions. This decision upset many doctors, who felt that the government was telling them how to practice medicine.

Two Who Changed the Rules

Before the 1960s, police officers and courts in the United States did not always respect certain rights of people who were arrested. In the 1960s, however, the U.S. Supreme Court wrote new rules about how police officers and courts should behave. The Court did this in two historic cases, known as *Gideon* and *Miranda*.

Gideon Calls for Justice

Someone had broken into a Florida poolroom in the summer of 1961. Bottles of Coke, beer, and wine were stolen. So was the money from two vending machines. A witness said he had seen Clarence Earl Gideon leaving the poolroom after the break-in—and Gideon had been found guilty of stealing in the past.

Gideon swore he was innocent. Too poor to pay a lawyer, Gideon asked the court to appoint one for him. The court said no. Florida courts provided free lawyers only when the defendant was facing the death penalty. Gideon's case wasn't that serious.

Gideon did his best to defend himself

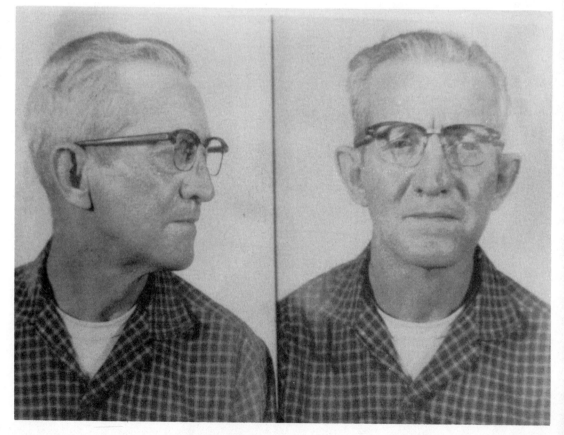

Clarence Gideon's case led the Supreme Court to rule that a lawyer must be provided for a defendant who can't afford to hire one.

but was found guilty of "breaking and entering." He got the longest possible sentence: five years in prison.

Gideon was very angry. He had led a hard life, and his health was poor. Those five years might be all he had left. He felt he might not have been sent to prison if he'd had a lawyer.

In prison, Gideon began reading law books to find a way out of his situation. In early 1962, he wrote to the U.S. Supreme Court. He asked that he be set free because he had been imprisoned illegally. The Supreme Court thought Gideon's case was important enough to hear, and it appointed lawyer Abe Fortas to argue the case for Gideon.

In 1963, Gideon won. The Court agreed that he had been denied his rights. Judge Hugo L. Black wrote that a person too poor to pay for a lawyer "cannot be assured of a fair trial unless counsel [a lawyer] is provided for him."

As a result of the ruling, all criminal defendants who cannot afford lawyers are provided with free counsel.

After nearly two years in prison, Clarence Gideon was a free man. "Do you feel like you accomplished something?" a reporter asked him. "Well, I did," Gideon said.

Thousands of American prisoners got new trials because of the *Gideon* decision. Since 1963, 35 states have created offices of "public defenders." The offices provide lawyers whose only job is to defend people who have been accused of a crime and can't afford lawyers. States that do not have public defenders pay lawyers to take on such cases.

Miranda

Ernesto A. Miranda had just finished working the night shift at a warehouse in Phoenix, Arizona. He went to bed.

Ernesto Miranda (right) with his lawyer. When he was arrested, the police did not inform Miranda of his rights as a suspect.

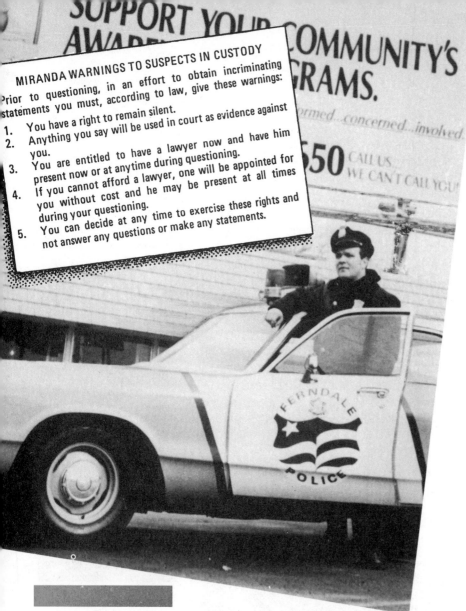

MIRANDA WARNINGS TO SUSPECTS IN CUSTODY

Prior to questioning, in an effort to obtain incriminating statements you must, according to law, give these warnings:

1. You have a right to remain silent.
2. Anything you say will be used in court as evidence against you.
3. You are entitled to have a lawyer now and have him present now or at anytime during questioning.
4. If you cannot afford a lawyer, one will be appointed for you without cost and he may be present at all times during your questioning.
5. You can decide at any time to exercise these rights and not answer any questions or make any statements.

Because of the *Miranda* decision, police must read suspects their rights.

What Ever Happened to Gideon and Miranda?

Both men got new trials, with different results. Gideon's lawyer proved him innocent. After Gideon was freed in 1963, he got a job, remarried, and began a new life. He lived in Florida until he died of cancer in 1972.

Miranda was again found guilty and got the same sentence. He was let out early, in 1972. Four years later, he was killed in a barroom fight over a card game.

An hour later, two police detectives woke him at his home. They took him to police headquarters. Then they questioned him about the kidnapping and rape of a local woman.

Within two hours, the sleepy Miranda said that he had committed that crime and others. He signed a confession that would later be used to convict him in court.

Miranda v. Arizona

Miranda appealed his conviction to the U.S. Supreme Court in *Miranda v. Arizona*. He pointed out that he had not been told of his right to remain silent during police questioning. Nor had he been told of his right to have a lawyer present. In 1966, the Court agreed that Miranda had been treated unfairly. It ruled in Miranda's favor.

The *Miranda* decision set new rules for the police. By law, police must read suspects their rights at the time of arrest. Suspects have the right to remain silent. Suspects also have the right to hire a lawyer or have one appointed for them.

At first, some police believed the *Miranda* decision would make their work harder and would free guilty suspects. Since then, however, police have grown used to it. It even gave them a new word. Police now ask each other, "Did you *Mirandize* him [read the suspect his rights]? " ■

During the 1960s and early 1970s, Supreme Court decisions often favored the individual citizen's rights. Roe v. Wade, Miranda v. Arizona, and the Gideon case are examples of the Court's stand on individual rights. Based on the current Court's stand on abortion, do you think the rights of the individual are still favored? Why or why not?

Stamp It "Secret"

In 1953, Congressman John E. Moss asked the Civil Service Commission for some information. The CSC is the agency that oversees government workers. To Moss's surprise, the CSC refused to send him the information he had asked for.

Moss couldn't believe it. He couldn't see any reason that the information should be kept secret. He decided to find out what gave the agency the right to withhold the information. He discovered that a 1946 law let agency heads declare any files they didn't want to share "off-limits." Moss fought to change that. His efforts helped to create a House Subcommittee on Government Information. Congressman Moss became chairman of this subcommittee.

The Freedom of Information Act

Moss and his subcommittee spent a decade pushing for a law that would give Americans more access to government information. The Freedom of Information Act finally cleared Congress, and President Johnson signed it into law on July 4, 1966. After FOIA went into effect, some famous people, including Dr. Martin Luther King, Jr., and John Lennon, learned that they had been spied on. The Federal Bureau of Investigation (FBI) had kept files on them.

Some information remains unavailable—defense secrets, for example. And not all FOIA requests are filled quickly. But for the most part, the FOIA put into law Americans' right to know. ∎

Civil rights leader Dr. Martin Luther King, Jr., (left) and ex-Beatle John Lennon were investigated by the FBI.

The Race to the MOON

"This nation should commit itself to achieving the goal, before this decade is out, of landing a man on the moon and returning him safely to Earth."
— *John F. Kennedy, Special Message to Congress, May 25, 1961*

Kennedy's message came just weeks after a great technological achievement. On May 5, 1961, Alan B. Shepard, Jr., had become the first U.S. astronaut to rocket into space. Shepard's 15-minute trip was a success. It carried him briefly into outer space, then back to Earth a few hundred miles from Cape Canaveral, where he had blasted off.

Blast-off of the *Friendship 7*. In 1962, John Glenn became the first American to orbit the Earth.

But he was not the first person to be launched into space. On April 12, 1961 – a month before Alan Shepard's flight – the Soviet Union's Yuri Gagarin had circled the globe. Kennedy and many other Americans feared that Gagarin's flight had put the United States hopelessly behind in the space race. Among them was Lieutenant Colonel John "Shorty" Powers, an American space official, who said, "We're all asleep. . . ." Other successful Soviet launches in 1961 made it look as if the Soviet lead was getting bigger. By the end of 1961, Soviet astronauts, called *cosmonauts,* had orbited the Earth many times. The United States had a lot of catching up to do.

FIVE CENTS

NEW YORK, WEDNESDAY, FEBRUARY 21, 1962.

VOL. CXI. No. 38,014.

GLENN ORBITS EARTH 3 TIMES SAFELY; PICKED UP IN CAPSULE BY DESTROYER; PRESIDENT WILL GREET HIM IN FLORIDA

81,000-MILE TRIP
Flight Aides Feared for the Capsule as It Began Its Re-Entry

Transcript of conversation with Glenn, Pages 26 and 34.

By RICHARD WITKIN

CARLINO CLEARED IN SHELTER CASE BY ETHICS PANEL
Lane Scored in Unanimous Report, Which He Calls 'Cynical and Callous'

Text of concluding sections of report is on Page 50.

By WARREN WEAVER Jr.

The Mercury Flights

The United States' first series of manned space flights was the Mercury program. On February 20, 1962, John Glenn, the third Mercury astronaut to blast off, circled the Earth three times in his *Friendship 7* space capsule. Americans sat glued to their TV sets during the mission. At one point, it looked as if Glenn might be in trouble. Viewers held their breath when it seemed that Glenn's capsule might burn up as it came back to Earth. When it came down safely, the country breathed a sigh of relief. Glenn's successful flight made Americans feel that they were still in the space race.

The Gemini Flights

Still, the Soviets continued to earn their own list of honors and space "firsts": the first woman in space, the first three-man crew, and the first space walk. (Cosmonauts were connected to the capsule by a cord.)

Then, starting in 1965, the Soviet space program appeared to stop for nearly 3½ years. During that period, the Soviets flew only one space mission. And that flight ended tragically. The cosmonaut died during the return to Earth. At some point during these years, the Soviet Union had apparently given up its dream of landing a man on the moon.

But the United States had never stopped trying. During 1965 and 1966, America made 10 successful flights under the Gemini program. The Gemini astronauts set a new record for length of time in space (nearly two weeks). They also performed a dazzling feat: "docking," or joining together, two spacecraft in orbit. Project Gemini's many successes paved the way for the third stage of the moon project: the Apollo program. Its flights would carry three astronauts, and it would take the United States to the moon.

"Fire in the Cockpit!"

On January 27, 1967, the *Apollo 1* spaceship stood on the launch pad at Cape Kennedy (formerly Cape Canaveral). It was being prepared for a flight in February. Three astronauts worked inside the spaceship, practicing a launch countdown. Suddenly, astronaut Gus Grissom shouted over the intercom, "Hey! Fire! We've got a fire in the cockpit!" Within seconds, the *Apollo 1* capsule was filled with flames. Gus Grissom, Edward White, and Roger Chaffee died before the ground crew could reach them.

The nation was stunned. Many people said that President Kennedy's dream of landing a man on the moon by the end of the 1960s was now impossible. But the space program's engineers went back to work to design a safer Apollo spacecraft. It took a year and a half and several unmanned Apollo flights for Americans to return to space. Finally, in October 1968, the first manned Apollo mission—*Apollo 7*—was ready to lift off. Kennedy's deadline for landing a man on the moon was only 14 months away.

U.S. astronaut Edward White in a "space walk," June 3, 1965. White later died in the January 1967 fire.

MEN WALK ON MOON

ASTRONAUTS LAND ON PLAIN; COLLECT ROCKS, PLANT FLAG

NEW YORK, MONDAY, JULY 21, 1969

CXVIII . No. 40,721

A Powdery Surface Is Closely E...

Voice From Moon: 'Eagle Has Landed'

EAGLE (the lunar module): Houston, Tranquility Base here. The Eagle has landed.
HOUSTON: Roger, Tranquility, we copy you on the ground. You've got a bunch of guys about to turn blue. We're breathing again. Thanks a lot.
TRANQUILITY BASE: Th...
HOUSTON: V...
TP...

The first Apollo astronauts took to the skies with a thundering roar on October 11, 1968. The spaceship's huge booster rocket rattled windows miles away as it lifted the ship through the Earth's atmosphere. People who watched the takeoff said they felt their insides vibrate from the shock wave.

The early manned Apollo missions (*Apollo 7* through *Apollo 10*) were successful. Two even orbited the moon. At last, the United States was ready to try a landing. *Apollo 11* blasted off on July 16, 1969.

The *Eagle* Lands

On July 20, the Lunar Excursion Module (LEM), nicknamed *Eagle*, landed on the moon. It carried astronauts Neil Armstrong and Edwin "Buzz" Aldrin. With them was a special video camera. Some 700 million television viewers around the world watched the shadowy image of Neil Armstrong leave the LEM. As Armstrong stood on the surface of the moon, he said: "That's one small step for man; one giant leap for mankind."

At the same time, the Soviets made a last effort to win the space race. If Armstrong and Aldrin had looked up, they could have seen *Luna 15* fly right over their moon base. This unmanned

---

Space Technology Comes to Earth

What do 747 jet airliners, swimming pools, and kitchen cookware have in common? They all use products or techniques that grew out of the U.S. space program.

Guidance systems were important to the success of the program. They kept spaceships on course during trips that covered hundreds of thousands of miles. The guidance systems and computers in today's jet airplanes owe much to those spacecraft systems. Electronic equipment that took astronauts to the moon and back now helps travelers by keeping jets on course.

The space program also led to new water-purifying systems. Scientists working for the Apollo program developed these systems

to provide astronauts with clean drinking water. Today, similar systems help clean polluted water and keep swimming pools clean.

Other products that grew out of space programs include sprays to prevent glasses from fogging, nonstick cookware, materials to protect us from fire, and information sent to Earth from satellites. This information has many uses. Photographs from satellites tell us about the condition of crops and forests. They also identify sources of pollution and help us locate natural resources. And no TV weather report would be complete without a satellite view of approaching storms. The space program continues to touch our lives in ways big and small.

Buzz Aldrin standing on the moon, July 20, 1969. About 700 million TV viewers watched the moon landing.

Soviet spacecraft was built to land on the moon, use a robot to gather moon rocks, and return to Earth before *Apollo 11*. But *Luna 15* crashed on the moon, ending Soviet hopes.

Four days later, the Apollo command module, nicknamed *Columbia,* landed in the Pacific Ocean. It and the astronauts it carried were picked up by United States Navy ships. President Kennedy did not live to see it, but his dream had become a reality. ■

Astronauts have not been to the moon since the last Apollo flight in 1972. Since that time, the United States has focused on unmanned flights that gathered scientific information and on the space shuttle program. But President Bush talked about ambitious future manned flights—including a landing on Mars. Do you think the United States should plan missions like this? Do you think they are good for the country? Do you think tax dollars should be spent on them?

Environmental Voices

Two environmental problems that many Americans became aware of during the 1960s: oil spills (above left) and air pollution (above right).

In 1962, a shy, quiet scientist named Rachel Carson wrote a book that shocked the nation. Carson's book, *Silent Spring*, sounded an alarm. It warned that DDT and other chemicals used to kill insects were harming plants and animals.

Many see Carson as the mother of modern-day environmentalism—the movement to protect the air, land, and water around us. *Silent Spring* made thousands of Americans aware of the damage people were doing to the planet. They began to agree with Carson that pollution was a major problem. So did the nation's leaders.

In May 1962, President Kennedy called a White House conference on conservation. Five hundred experts attended. In 1965, President Johnson hosted a White House conference on natural beauty. His wife, the popular Lady Bird Johnson, urged Americans to protect the natural beauty of the land. White House conferences like these helped get more people thinking about the environment—and how they might care for it.

Oil Disaster

In fact, throughout the 1960s, more and more people were becoming aware of air, water, and soil pollution. Newspapers, magazines, and television began giving more coverage to pollution problems facing the United States. One incident that received national attention was the Santa Barbara oil spill. In 1969, an oil well off the southern California coast – near the city of Santa Barbara – spilled thousands of gallons of oil into the Pacific Ocean. Beaches near Santa Barbara were covered with thick black goo. Thousands of birds and other animals were killed. Hundreds of Californians and others pitched in to help clean up the mess.

New Laws

In the early 1960s, the U.S. government had passed laws protecting the environment. But now, as environmental issues grew more important, the government became much more active in creating pollution laws and making sure that they were followed. In 1969, Congress voted the National Environmental Policy Act (NEPA) into law. The act set up new guidelines for industries to follow when disposing of toxic (poisonous) waste. NEPA also said that before highways, dams, and other federal projects are built, the government agency in charge must prepare an environmental impact statement. This report must explain how the project could harm the environment. In 1970, the Environmental Protection Agency (EPA) was created to make sure that companies that had been polluting would follow the new rules.

More laws to protect the environment followed quickly. The Endangered Species Act made it a crime to kill animals that were in danger of becoming extinct. The Clean Air Act and the Clean Water Act strengthened laws to control pollution. In 1972, the government greatly restricted the use of DDT. Rachel Carson's warning of 10 years before had finally been heeded.

Around the World

People in other countries also were worried about the environment. Governments in Africa and Asia were concerned about high birthrates and overcrowding. Many countries did not have enough food and water to go around. The environment could not support a high birthrate. In Europe, water and air pollution were hurting people as well as the environment. Acid rain was killing forests, and heavy smog was increasing lung disease. In 1972, the United Nations held the Conference on the Human Environment to talk about solving these problems. It was the first international meeting to discuss ways to protect the environment.

Selected Federal Environmental Legislation 1961–1975

Name of Law	Year Enacted	Description
Clean Air Act	1963	Gave federal government control over air pollution that affected more than one state.
Clean Water Restoration Act	1966	Provided federal government money for building water treatment plants.
Air Quality Act	1967	Set standards for air quality.
National Environmental Policy Act (NEPA)	1969	Made "productive harmony between man and the environment" a national policy. Said that all federal projects had to consider their impact on the environment. Established the Council on Environmental Quality.
Water Quality Improvement Act	1970	Banned dumping oil in waters traveled by ships. Required plans for cleaning spills.
Clean Air Act	1970	Required standards for clean air. Gave Environmental Protection Agency power to enforce laws.
Federal Environmental Pesticide Control Act	1972	Set up rules for making and using pesticides.
Noise Control Act	1972	Set up noise standards and research on the effects of noise pollution
Safe Drinking Water Act	1974	Set up standards for taste, odor, and appearance of water. Made a survey of rural drinking water quality.

As people became aware of the pollution problem, many began protesting for changes.

Tough Choices

Though environmentalists made progress, it did not come easily. For example, chemical companies and some of the people who used their products said that Rachel Carson's research for *Silent Spring* was full of mistakes. In addition, lumber and oil companies said we had a tough choice to make. If we put limits on logging or exploring for oil, thousands of people would lose their jobs.

Americans began to face other tough choices. They liked big, fast cars. But the cars used a lot of gasoline and polluted the air. Would Americans be willing to give up their bigger cars for cleaner air? Also, cleaning the environment cost money. Would Americans be willing to pay higher taxes for improvements like better sewage treatment systems? Questions like these were not easy to answer.

But the big change was that Americans were asking these questions at all. By the mid-1970s, many Americans had begun to pay attention to the environment – and few politicians dared to ignore environmental problems. ■

Protecting the environment is everyone's responsibility. What have you done to protect it? You might check with your town's chamber of commerce to see what people in your community are doing.

Suppose that you live in an area where many people are out of work. A company plans to build a factory that will create hundreds of new jobs for your community. But the factory will also harm wildlife in your area. Would you be in favor of the factory? Why or why not?

THEN & NOW

On April 22, 1970, a new kind of demonstrator appeared by the millions across America. These people were not demonstrating for civil rights or against the war in Vietnam. They were speaking out against pollution and for the environment.

That first Earth Day was more than demonstrations. At schools and universities, citizens and their leaders held hundreds of "teach-ins." They discussed problems of pollution, pesticides, population growth, and nuclear power. They began to think about solutions for saving endangered animals and protecting wilderness areas.

At the 20th Earth Day in 1990, some of the issues had changed. The big concerns were the destruction of the rain forest, the need for clean air, and the greenhouse effect – the gradual warming of the earth. Some older issues, such as whether to use nuclear power, remained. But the environmental movement could point to real progress in cleaning up America's air and water.

The Decade of the Heart

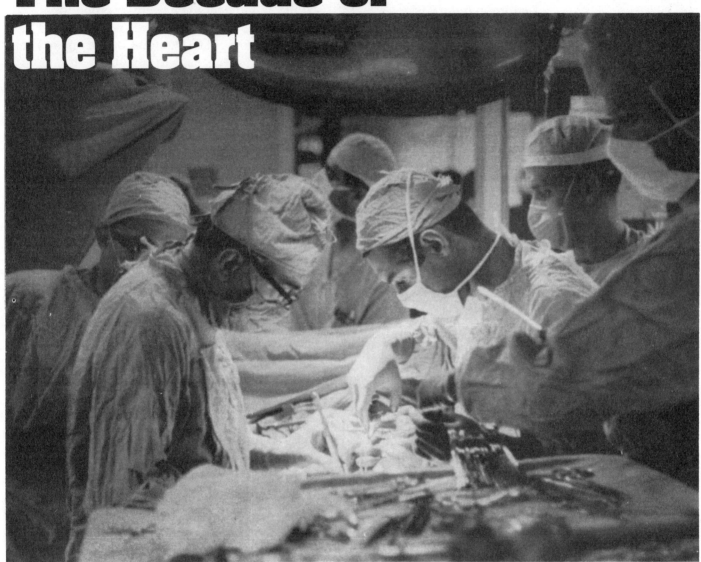

Heart disease has long been the number-one killer of Americans. But death rates from heart disease have been dropping steadily since the 1960s. During that decade, scientists found ways to fight heart disease that would have seemed like magic just a few years before.

Surgeons developed new methods for repairing damaged hearts. They also found ways to treat clogged arteries. If the arteries were not treated, blood

would be unable to flow through them, and the heart would stop. Doctors found ways for blood to travel around the clogged arteries – to "bypass" them.

In 1967, Dr. Rene Favaloro performed the first bypass operation ever done on a human being. He removed a piece of a vein from a patient's leg and then attached it above and below the blocked part in the artery. Now, blood could flow around the block and use the new vein to

In 1968, doctors in Houston, Texas, performing one of the first heart transplants.

reach the heart. By the mid-1970s, surgeons were performing this operation regularly.

Studies in the 1960s pointed to a major cause of heart disease: smoking. In 1965, the government required cigarette makers to put health warnings on cigarette packs. And by 1971, TV and radio cigarette ads were banned. Doctors urged their patients to quit smoking.

Unfortunately, for some patients, quitting smoking and even bypass surgery were not enough. Their hearts were too damaged. By the end of the 1960s, a new hope appeared for these patients: the heart transplant. Patients were given new hearts, usually taken from healthy people who had died suddenly. Dr. Christiaan Barnard, in South Africa, performed the first human heart transplant on December 3, 1967. Three days later, Dr. Adrian Kantrowitz performed the first U.S. heart transplant.

The first transplant patients did not survive long. But surgeons quickly gained more experience. And chemists developed powerful drugs to prevent the body from rejecting the new heart. By the mid-1970s, heart transplants had become a useful method for helping a patient whose heart was failing. Dr. Denton Cooley, one of the first surgeons to perform heart transplants, later reminisced about the pathfinding heart surgeons of the 1960s and 1970s. He wrote, "Without such pioneering spirit, many of the diseases and defects that affect the heart would not have been conquered." ■

The heart is not the only body part that is being transplanted today by surgeons. Livers, kidneys, and corneas have been transplanted successfully. People can fill out and carry "organ donor cards." These cards say that those carrying one want their organs removed after they die and given to others.

Would you like to donate your organs to help someone live? Why or why not?

Would you sign a form to donate a loved one's organs? Why or why not?

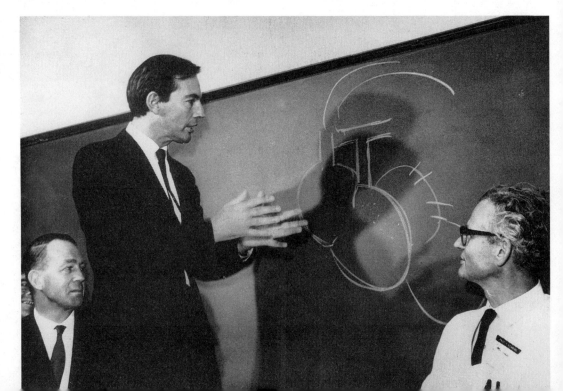

Dr. Christiaan Barnard (standing) explaining how he performed the world's first heart transplant.

* This symbol before a page number indicates a photograph of the subject mentioned.

Credits

Photo Credits

Courtesy Academy of Motion Picture Arts and
Sciences: 51b
Courtesy Atlanta Braves: 57
The Bettmann Archives: 6, 7, 8, 9, 10, 12, 13, 14,
20b, 21, 22, 23, 25, 27, 29, 30, 31, 32, 33, 34, 37,
38ab, 40, 50, 51a, 52, 55, 59b, 60, 61, 62ab, 63,
69ab, 70, 72, 73, 74a, 76, 77, 79, 81, 83ab, 90, 92
Courtesy The Courier-Journal: 64, 65
Courtesy Fairchild Books, Division Fairchild
Group, NY: 41
Courtesy Los Angeles Dodgers, Inc.: 58
Courtesy Lyndon Baines Johnson Library: 75
Courtesy NASA: 84, 85
Courtesy National Automotive History Collection,
Detroit Public Library: 82
Courtesy National Park Service: 18
Newark Public Library, Newark, NJ: 2a, 36
Panama City, FL, News Herald: 80
Photofest: 39, 44, 46, 47acd, 48a
Smithsonian Institution Photo #73-2089: 20a
University of Kansas Archives: 59a
United Press International: 74b
U.S. Army Photograph: 49
Courtesy Watergate Hotel: 24

Text Credits

The quotations on page 43 are reprinted with
permission of Atheneum Publishers, an imprint
of Macmillan Publishing Company, from
American Beat by Bob Greene. Copyright ©
1983 by John Deadline Enterprises, Inc.
The poetry on page 54 from *The Greatest: My Own
Story* is reprinted by permission of Muhammad
Ali.
The words from "We Shall Overcome" on page 75
(by Z. Horton, F. Hamilton, G. Carawan, P.
Seeger) are reprinted with permission. Copyright
© 1960 (renewed) and 1963 (renewed) Ludlow
Music, Inc., New York, NY.